FROM LOCHNAW
TO MANITOULIN

FROM LOCHNAW TO MANITOULIN

A Highland Soldier's Tour Through Upper Canada

EDITED BY
SCOTT A. MCLEAN

NATURAL HERITAGE BOOKS

TORONTO

Published by Natural Heritage/Natural History Inc.
P.O. Box 95, Station O, Toronto, Ontario M4A 2M8

Design by Blanche Hamill, Norton Hamill Design
Edited by Jane Gibson
Printed and bound in Canada by Hignell Printing Limited

Canadian Cataloguing in Publication Data

Agnew, Andrew, Sir, 1818–1892
From Lochnaw to Manitoulin: a highland soldier's tour through
Upper Canada

Includes bibliographical references and index.
ISBN 1-896219-56-X

1. Agnew, Andrew, Sir, 1818-1892. 2. Great Britain. Army. Sutherland Highlanders. 3. Ontario—History—1791-1841. 4. Indians of North America—
Ontario—Manitoulin Island—Government relations. 5. Ontario—Description
and travel. I. McLean, Scott A. (Scott Alan), 1963- . Title.

FC3071.A45 1999   971.3'.02   C99-931718-0
F1058.A45 1999

THE CANADA COUNCIL | LE CONSEIL DES ARTS
FOR THE ARTS | DU CANADA
SINCE 1957 | DEPUIS 1957

Natural Heritage Books acknowledges the support received for its publishing
program from the Canada Council Block Grant Program. Also acknowledged
is the assistance of the Association for the Export of Canadian Books, Ottawa.
Natural Heritage Books acknowledges the support of the Ontario Arts
Council for its publishing program.

This work is dedicated to Carly and Connor,
my own wee travellers
with a taste for adventure.

Acknowledgments

There are many people who have played a part in bringing this work to completion. I would first and foremost like to thank the Agnew family and, in particular, Sir Crispin Agnew, for his kind permission to publish his great-grandfather's journal. I would also like to thank Dr. Carl Benn for feedback on an earlier manuscript and the publisher, Barry Penhale, and editor, Jane Gibson, for their continued interest, involvement and enthusiasm for the project. The archivists at the University of Guelph Library, the Scottish Record Office and Michigan State Archives were all extremely helpful tracking down information and illustrations. Special thanks go to Dr. Scott Moir, for his assistance 'filling in some gaps,' to Ruth McCartney, for her much needed 'technological support' and to Dr. Rosamund M. Vanderburgh for her help in extending the profiles of Native leaders of the time. And finally, I would like to thank my brother Steve, who made a necessary research trip to Michigan an exceptionally enjoyable experience.

While every effort has been made to ensure the accuracy of information in this book, any corrections or suggestions will be gratefully received for incorporation in future editions.

Contents

Preface

It is often the case that a particular line of study leads the researcher down unexpected and fruitful paths. Such is the case with the present work. While completing course work for a Masters degree in Scottish History at the University of Guelph, I was required to rummage through the archives in search of documents which had never been studied, and then write a paper on what I had uncovered. I chanced upon a *Record of the Services of the 93rd (or Sutherland) Highland Regiment of Foot*, written by a Captain Charles Gordon while he was stationed in the West Indies in 1830.

The document begins with a brief narrative of the early history of the regiment from its inception in 1799. From 1809, when Charles Gordon, then an Ensign, joined the regiment, the document relates first-hand experience. Gordon's account of the regiment's role in the Battle of New Orleans was particularly compelling. There, the 93rd took heavy losses against a well-fortified American force and Gordon himself was severely wounded in the cheek. I was hooked.

The study of this one document led to a greater interest in the 93rd Highlanders. I was both surprised and extremely intrigued to find that the regiment had served in Upper Canada from 1838 to 1848, a most interesting time in Canadian history. Research into the regiment during its service in Upper Canada brought me upon a significant collection of documents, the "Lochnaw Muniments," housed at the Scottish Record Office in Edinburgh. The collection includes a variety of letters, a diary and a journal kept by Lieutenant Andrew Agnew of Lochnaw, who served with the 93rd from 1835 to 1842. Lieutenant Agnew's correspondence with his family back in Scotland provided a wealth of information on the 93rd Highlanders, military life in a colonial garrison and the regiment's part in the defence of Canada . One document in particular caught my eye. It was a journal he kept while travelling to Manitoulin Island to attend the annual gift-giving ceremony between government representatives and Native leaders. Lieutenant Agnew's colourful descriptions of the men and women, including the Native peoples he met, the settlements and the flora and fauna encountered en route, made it a document which I felt others should have the opportunity to read.

Editor's Introduction

Andrew Agnew (1818-1892), the author of the journal documenting a tour to Manitoulin, was the eldest of one of Southern Scotland's prominent families. The Agnews of Lochnaw have a long association with Wigtonshire, for generations being actively involved in the political, social and religious development of the region in particular, and of Scotland in general. Andrew Agnew Sr., Andrew's father, served the county as Member of Parliament and was a vocal advocate for the observance of the Sabbath. Some time later, Andrew himself represented the county in parliament, after he had succeeded his father as Eighth Baronet of Lochnaw in 1849, but not before he had embarked upon a career in the military.

For many members of the Scottish landed class, a military career offered great opportunity for advancement and travel abroad. With this in mind, Andrew Agnew joined the 93rd Highland Regiment of Foot in 1835 at the age of seventeen. At that time, the regiment was stationed in Ireland, but would soon leave for Canada to strengthen the British garrisons against the threat of Rebellion. Agnew began his military career at the rank of Ensign, and was promoted to Lieutenant on the 29th of September 1837. He made Captain in 1841, before transferring to the 4th Light Dragoons in 1842.

In the years following the close of the Napoleonic Wars in 1815, Britain and its colonies experienced widespread movements for reform. In Upper Canada, as in Britain itself, efforts at reform were opposed by those in power, still fearful of a revolution of the type which had broken out in France decades earlier. When a Fifeshire Scot named Robert Gourlay arrived in Upper Canada

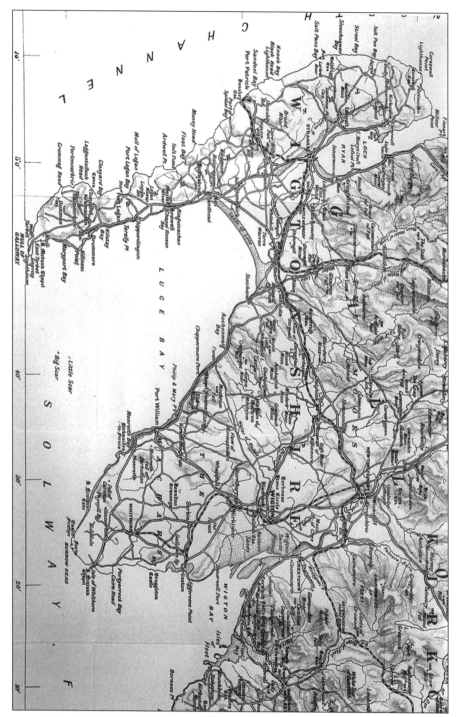

Map of Wigtonshire circa 1916 showing the location of Lochnaw to the west of Stranraer, in the southwestern most point of Scotland. From Rev. C. H. Dick, *Highways and Byways in Galloway and Carrick*. London: 1924.

in 1817 with a mind to promote British settlement in the province, he found that most of the land was controlled by the clergy, government officials and their friends.[1] Gourlay concluded that the Family Compact,[2] a close-knit group with similar interests that dominated the province, had to be challenged and the system reformed. A very stubborn individual and a forceful speaker, Gourlay gained wide support, but also alienated a number of the more powerful men in the province with his criticisms of the government's land policies. Twice charges of sedition were brought against him and twice he successfully defended himself. However, a third arrest led to a lengthy period in jail and banishment from Upper Canada. Gourlay's challenge to the Family Compact was unsuccessful, but it attracted others to his cause.[3]

The push for reform took a new turn in 1820 when another Scot, William Lyon Mackenzie, settled in Upper Canada. Mackenzie initially set up shop as a druggist and bookseller in York, near King and Yonge Streets. He later bought out his partner, John Lesslie, and moved to Queenston near Niagara Falls. Soon after, he began publishing the *Colonial Advocate*, which he used as a platform to attack the colonial government.[4] Under Mackenzie's fervent guidance the reform movement spread and, by 1835, open rebellion seemed a distinct possibility.

Similar grumbling was occurring in Lower Canada where the movement was led by the capable Louis Joseph Papineau.[5] An 1832 by-election in Montreal ended in a riot in which soldiers opened fire on the crowd, killing three and wounding two others. "Patriote" newspapers cried out at the injustice of the act and fanned the flames of rebellion. By the spring of 1837, rebellion was in the air and Papineau and his followers had made contact with Mackenzie at York. Their plan called for a simultaneous uprising in both provinces, Papineau hoping that Mackenzie would keep the British Regulars at Kingston from moving east to the defence of the Lower Province. Great Britain responded quickly, sending nine regiments of regular troops, a detachment

William Lyon Mackenzie (1795–1861), a native of
Scotland, emigrated to Canada in 1820. His newspaper, the *Colonial Advocate*, strongly condemned
the provincial government of the time. In 1828,
Mackenzie was elected to the legislative assembly
and became the leader of radical reformers. Following the 1837 Rebellion, he lived in the United States,
returning to Canada in 1850 following a pardon
granted to him by Queen Victoria. *Heritage Toronto*.
From *Historic Fort York* by Carl Benn.

of Royal Marines and 200 sailors into Upper Canada to quell the
rebellion and restore order. On November 24th William Lyon
Mackenzie rode out from Toronto to muster his 'army' and on
December 5th began his 'March' on Toronto City Hall.[6] The rebel
resistance at Montgomery's Tavern was short-lived, Mackenzie
taking flight to Niagara and across the border. The rebellion in
Lower Canada met with much the same result. This rebellion,
although having greater popular support, was easily put down

while Papineau and several other of the leaders also fled south of the border. What followed in both provinces has been described as a "witch hunt," where anyone sympathetic to reform was persecuted and forced to flee to the border states.[7]

By December of 1837, it appeared that the threat of rebellion had passed, yet the danger was far from over. The severity of the persecutions of the rebels left many extremely bitter and willing to continue fighting from the safety of the United States. Mackenzie had arrived at Buffalo on December 11th and immediately set about recruiting a 'patriot army.'[8] A more serious threat was posed by the 'Brotherhood of Hunters,' a secret organization founded by an American, Robert Nelson, dedicated to fighting for the liberation of Canada. Despite a proclamation of neutrality issued by the United States President Van Buren,[9] the Hunters were able to secure 1 000 U.S. Army muskets and three field guns. The organization grew at an incredible rate and preparations were made for an invasion into Upper Canada.[10] Initial raids at Amherstburg and across Lake Erie via the ice were easily turned away, and a raid by Robert Nelson into Lower Canada saw his force chased back to Vermont. Tension along the border mounted throughout the winter months of 1838 and, with the threat of further raids and reports of disharmony within Lower Canada, the British government reinforced the strength of the army with two additional regiments, one of which was the 93rd Regiment of Foot. Ongoing accounts of the dispersion of the recruitment of the 93rd have demonstrated how the regiment relied heavily upon Sutherland men during the two decades after its foundation.[11] R. H. Burgoyne, who wrote a history of the regiment in 1883, believed that the recruitment of men from a limited region of Scotland had instilled a high level of character into the regimental members.

Not only were many of the non-commissioned officers and privates the children of respectable farmers, and almost all of them of reputable parentage, but a certain proportion of the officers themselves were gentlemen associated with the counties in which the battalion was recruited. Both they and the soldiers regarded the regiment as one large family bound together by the strong ties of neighbourhood, and even of relationship.[12] The regiment was initially organised into platoons and companies by parish of origin, a fact which Henderson argues brought about a significant degree of social control.[13] However, from the 1820s on the composition of the 93rd, and of all Highland Regiments, changed significantly as the army was forced to look farther afield for new recruits.[14]

Initially the regiment saw limited action, being stationed in Scotland, Ireland and, in 1806, in the Cape of Good Hope. It was not until being sent to America that the mettle of the regiment was, for the first time, severely tested at the Battle of New Orleans in 1814. Captain Charles Gordon, who was seriously wounded in the engagement, gave the following account:

> "The left column...continued advancing with the eager and sanguine hopes of pushing forward and forcing the Enemy's Lines, when just as it had got nearly within Musket Range orders were given for each Corps to form into close Columns again and await under the best shelter (where in point of fact there was little or none) for further orders to advance, but for this order which was so fondly and momentarily. Anticipated, they waited in vain being kept under fire for five hours."[15]

Here, holding its position while under heavy fire, the regiment gained its high reputation for discipline and bravery.

Following the close of the Napoleonic War in 1815, Britain's need for a large military force was greatly reduced. Many regiments were disbanded or reduced in size at this time. From 1815 to 1838, the 93rd was largely occupied with routine garrison duties in Ireland, England and the West Indies. In 1837, the regiment was stationed in Ireland where it was preparing for service overseas, and it appeared likely that it would be sent to Gibraltar. However, with the spread of rebellion in Canada, the 93rd received orders in late December 1837, to disembark for Halifax. On January 6th, 1838, the ship *Inconstant* left Cork harbour with nine officers and 250 men and began the voyage overseas. On January 23rd the remainder of the regiment, under Lieutenant-Colonel MacGregor, embarked in the frigate, the *Pique*.[16]

The ships landed safely in Halifax where the regiment began preparations for its part in the defence of the Canadas. While in British North America the regiment was stationed throughout Upper and Lower Canada, from Quebec City to Toronto, with a number of small companies briefly serving in Prince Edward Island and Cape Breton. The regiment would remain in the colonies until 1848, long after the threat of rebellion had ended.

While stationed in British North America, the men of the 93rd were confronted with the hardships of garrison duty in the colonies. A soldier's life during the 1830s and 1840s could be exceedingly difficult; the rigors, monotony and boredom of garrison duty presented challenges to both officers and the rank and file. Barracks were generally crowded, in various states of repair and suffered immensely from a government trying to curb spending. Food was the least of the common soldier's worries. By the 1830s, many regiments were adding a third meal to the soldiers' diet which already included one pound of meat and one pound of bread per day. The portions were sufficient, although lacking in fruits and vegetables. The problem was, like the rest of garrison life, the monotony, as little effort was put into food preparation.[17] The blandness of the food was compensated by the availability of alcohol. It was common practice to supply troops with a daily ration of alcohol which some believed helped to "sustain and invigorate" the men. In Britain, troops received 1d a day beer money while those serving in colonial garrisons received a daily ration of beer, wine or rum.[18] Drunkenness itself was a serious problem within the British military but perhaps of more concern

Officers' Dress. Illustration is from R. H. Burgoyne, *Historical Records of the 93rd Sutherland Highlanders* (1883).

was the lack of discipline and other offences associated with it.[19]

Any sort of transgression could be expected to be met with harsh discipline. The lash was still in use, although by the 1830s public pressure and the changing attitudes of commanders had greatly reduced reliance on corporal punishment.[20] However, throughout the 1830s and 1840s there was a growing movement towards prevention through provision of alternatives, and the creation of a more 'moral' soldier. Greater effort was placed upon the soldier's spiritual welfare, education and health.[21] The men of the 93rd were fortunate to be commanded by Colonel Sparks, who strongly believed in the efficacy of providing for his men. As early as November 1839, Colonel Sparks was working to establish a savings bank for the men of the 93rd.[22] The 93rd was also one of the first regiments to benefit from the establishment of a regimental library.[23]

Despite efforts to improve the life of the British soldier, the poor living conditions, strict discipline and meagre pay still induced many to turn to desertion, a significant problem for which military leaders had few answers. Officers seem to have been at a loss as to how they could effectively control the number of deserters. In a letter regarding the prevention of desertion one officer stated that, in his opinion:

> "...it would be extremely difficult to adopt any <u>measure</u> for preventing desertion in this command owing to the situation of the country, bordering as it does on the long line of frontier of the United States, which not only holds out great inducements to the soldiers from the constant ideas indulged in by them of bettering their condition from the high rate of wages supposed to be given them there...particularly those who have been brought up to any trade."[24]

Some blamed the Irish for the high rate of desertion, suggesting that they "...are induced to desert from their having relations and friends settled in various parts of the U.S. and no doubt many Irish enlist for no other purpose than that of ultimately affecting this objective, and being brought to America free of expense."[25] The 93rd, although known for its discipline, did not escape the increase in desertions taking place. Each year a small number of men attempted escape and in 1847 six men deserted. Those rank and file viewed as potential deserters were sent to Penetanguishene, where escape was not so easy. As well, another four men, including one sergeant, were stationed there in order to prevent any such attempts. From January 1848 to June 1848 a total of nine men deserted from the regiment. After June there were no more desertions as the regiment received orders to return to Scotland in September.

While the monotony of garrison duties was the norm, the 93rd did see some limited action in the battle of Windmill Point at Prescott, Upper Canada. On Sunday, November 11, a party of about 400 Patriots, after being stirred by the rhetoric of William Lyon Mackenzie and others, crossed the St. Lawrence from Ogdensburg to 'liberate' the Canadians from British rule. Their plan was to take Fort Wellington, on the east side of Prescott, however, poor navigation and planning led to their coming aground below the windmill at the small settlement of New Jerusalem.[26] Once fortified in the windmill and surrounding houses, the Patriots settled in to wait for the expected reinforcements. They did not arrive.

The Patriots, led by Nils von Schoultz,[27] soon found themselves surrounded by local militia and regular troops from Fort Henry. The 93rd arrived on November 16th and "took their place on the Prescott side but almost fronting the mill..."[28] The thickness of the windmill walls protected the Patriots and made the regiments work most difficult. It was not until several 18 pound cannon and a howitzer were deployed that the Patriots "courage began to fail."[29] On November 17th, after the battle had ended, the Kingston newspaper reported that 102 Patriots had been killed and 162 taken prisoner.[30] For Lieutenant Agnew and the men of the 93rd, the battle was a welcome diversion from garrison duty. Lieutenant Agnew states that the end of the battle "...was a fine sight, the flames throwing a rich gleam over the bayonets...and the darkness adding much to the effect...Our other companies came

Windmill Point, Prescott. Today the site of the Battle of the Windmill bears little resemblance to what it was in 1838. In 1879, the windmill was converted into a lighthouse, and the hamlet of New Jerusalem has all but disappeared. It is still, however, possible to gain a sense of the formidable position it represented. *Courtesy National Archives of Canada.*

up next morning much disappointed at being too late."[31]

The Battle of the Windmill was the only military action the 93rd was to see while stationed in Upper Canada. Like many other regiments, much of their time was spent assisting the civic authorities. One example is their policing role during the election to the Provincial Assembly in Montreal in 1844. On the second day of polling, a riot was incited by 300 to 400 men from the canals at Lachine. The disturbance continued until a party of the 93rd was ordered to charge, dispersing the crowd and sending thirty to jail.[32] The 93rd was also instrumental in putting out the Griffintown Fire in Montreal in 1845. The fire threatened to engulf much of the city and, in the end, left 109 families homeless. In an effort to contain the spread of the blaze, the 93rd blew up several buildings.[33] Montreal city council expressed its "very

The proximity of the military establishment at Old Fort Henry ensured that Highland soldiers would play a prominent role in the social life of Kingston. W. H. Bartlett in Willis' *Canadian Scenery*. Volume II. 1848. *Special Collections, University of Guelph.*

high sense entertained...of their [the 93rd's] unremitting and meritorious services and the invaluable aid given by them."[34]

A Highland Regiment could have an impact upon the colonies simply by its presence. The presence of a regiment offered a sense of security, while the kilted soldiers on Sunday parade presented a welcomed spectacle. The officers in particular mixed with the higher social circles of the colonies, attending dinners, socials and the theatre, all of which brought an added sense of cultural refinement and colour to the colonies. As John Philp so rightly pointed out, "...the British Army had a share in shaping the social and economic growth of that nation. Each garrison was a link with Empire..."[35]

Like the rank and file serving under him, Lieutenant Agnew had to persevere through the drudgery and hardships associated with garrison duty in British North America. Within his correspondence can be found complaints regarding the constant removal from one post to another, such as happened after a recent march into Lower Canada, "...when to our great disgust we were ordered back to Upper Canada...we were to have three days to rest."[36] Other complaints included the boredom, muddy roads, poor weather and general lack of supplies which must have plagued most regardless of rank.[37] However, as an officer, Lieutenant Agnew had options available to him which the rank and file did not. Apart from the obvious opportunities to mix socially with the civilian population and attendance at a wide variety of functions, it was also possible for officers to be granted extended leaves of absence where they might travel abroad or return home to attend to personal affairs. In July of 1839, Lieutenant Agnew wrote home to inform his family that he had been granted a two month leave of absence so that he might join a party going to Manitoulin Island for the annual gift-giving ceremony.

Gift-giving ceremonies were a common feature of British-Native relations during the 17th and 18th centuries, when such rituals were used to ensure peaceful relations and military support. In the 1830s, this practice was continued, ensuring positive alliances and facilitating the surrender of new territories. In 1836, the Ojibwa of the Saugeen Peninsula surrendered 1.5 million acres, with further land being surrendered over the following decades. Manitoulin Island emerged as a centre for Native re-settlement, a place Lieutenant-Governor Sir Francis Bond Head deemed safe from the damaging influence of 'civilization.'[38] Each year approximately 1,500 Natives from throughout the northern Great Lakes Basin would gather to receive gifts: copper kettles, rifles, knives, gunpowder and shot, clothes, needles and other items, representing a total value of about £800.

Lieutenant Agnew's party's role was to assist in the gift-giving and "impress the natives with the grandeur of the British Military."[39] Of the six other men, some, like Agew, were officers attached to regiments, some were political representatives. The trip was going to be more pleasure than business, affording the party ample time to enjoy what the region had to offer. Agnew enthusiastically related to his father that they would be going "...up Georgian Bay in large canoes, camping every night and landing if we see any good shooting or any chance of amusement."[40] Lieutenant Agnew was clearly excited about the prospects for adventure the trip offered and this enthusiasm is clearly displayed in the journal he kept.

A wide range of travellers journeyed through Upper Canada during the early decades of the nineteenth century, describing the land, people and events which they encountered. Well-known figures like John Galt, Adam Ferguson and Francis Bond Head wrote substantial accounts of their travels in Upper Canada. Anna Jameson's *Winter Studies and Summer Rambles in Canada* (1839) is particularly relevant to the present work as Lieutenant Andrew Agnew followed much the same route during his sojourn through Upper Canada and refers to Mrs. Jameson on several occasions. Other lesser known figures like William Thomson, author of *A Tradesman's Travels in the United States and Canada*, and countless emigrants writing home to tell family and friends their story or encourage them to emigrate, provide unique descriptions of Upper Canada and what it offered settlers, tradesman and others in search of a new beginning.

The journal of Andrew Agnew of Lochnaw has similarities with this larger body of travel literature, but there are also important differences which make the document an important source for the period. As with other examples of travel literature, Lieutenant Agnew spends considerable time describing the landscape along with the flora and fauna he encountered. He was clearly impressed with Native culture: their behaviour, appearance, and skill with a canoe, all of which he describes in detail and with an obvious sense of fascination. The detail with which he describes the gift-giving ceremony on Manitoulin alone makes his journal an important source for British/Native

A Settler's Hut on the Frontier. W. H. Bartlett in Willis' *Canadian Scenery*. Volume II. 1848. *Special Collections, University of Guelph.*

relations. Yet, the journal's value as a source of history goes much further. As the journal was written by an officer of an Highland Regiment and a member of Scotland's landed class, the journal provides a unique perspective into those things which were of interest to an officer serving in the colonies. Descriptions of wildlife focus largely upon hunting, a favourite pastime of the British landed class. A sense of pleasure is betrayed whenever a 'gentleman' is met with or a good bottle of brandy or port available. In short, Lieutenant Angew's journal offers insight into the attitudes and expectations of a British officer stationed in British North America. It provides evidence of the officer gentleman tradition perpetuated by the British Army throughout the nineteenth century.

Unlike much of the travel literature available, the present work was not published. It was a personal journal kept by an officer and was meant to be read by his immediate friends and family. The language, therefore, has a personal tone to it as the author is describing circumstances and events which he deemed of interest. As the original is in manuscript form, the journal reads quite differently than a published account which might be embellished or edited at a later date. The original manuscript, which is housed at the Scottish Record Office in Edinburgh, is in a varying state of preservation. Where possible, the journal has been kept in its original form. However, due to damaged or non-legible sections, there are areas of the manuscript where words or phrases are missing. Where this is the case, a blank has been left to indicate a missing word or combination of words. Minimal changes have been made to spelling and grammar in order to ensure that it reflects, as accurately as possible, the original document.

A Tour to Manitoulin, 1839

The Journal of Lieutenant Andrew Agnew

Lieutenant Andrew Agnew, age 21, along with a party of six men, leaves Toronto on Friday, July 19th en route to Manitoulin Island to take part in the annual gift-giving with the assembly of Native Peoples in early August. The total journey, by stagecoach, canoe and train, takes eight weeks. Agnew, with his companions, arrives back in Toronto on September 16, 1839.

This is his journal.

Friday 19 July

Started at 10 O'clock A.M. by coach to St. Albans[1] (formerly Beverley). Our party consisted of Col. Spark, Lieut. Buchanan and myself (93rd) Meade and Hon. T Lindsay (43rd) and Baker (73) and Stuart. Beautiful day but very hot. Changed horses at Richmond Hill. Half way very hard work for the horses, what would Mr. Martin say? Got a very good luncheon at the Inn, and drove on taking the second team through to St. Albans. Macadamization[2] ceased 10 miles out of Toronto, but from the soil being light and sandy the road is very tolerable although very narrow. Passed through New Market, a pretty little village. 32 miles from Toronto and arrived at the S.A. Inn in 8 hours and 40 minutes—36 miles. The driving down hill was occasionally quite horrific, no drags! Let em away and take care of yourselves! Mr. Jarvis the protector of the Indians[,] 2 sons, a Mr. Snider and Mr. Georgian came up here and completed the party.

20 July

On by coach 9 ___ miles to Holland River and started in the Simcoe steamer at 1/4 after 8,—7 miles down the river, most interesting appearance from immense extent of marsh with occasional rice ponds on each bank and thick bush beyond. Called at

1 St. Albans, later known as Holland Landing, was located on Yonge Street, north of Toronto.
2 This term refers to the Scottish inventor John L. McAdam, born in Ayr, who developed the process of covering a road with small broken stones compressed to form pavement. McAdam had journeyed to New York City in 1770, where he made a fortune in his uncle's counting house. Upon his return to Scotland in 1783, he began experimenting with new types of road construction. In recognition of his work he was made Surveyor General of Metropolitan Roads in Great Britain in 1827.

Detail of map of Upper Canada, a sketch to show "the Practicable courses of the GRAND COMMERCIAL CANAL OF ST. LAWRENCE with its Junctions." Andrew Agnew's route (1839) can be traced going north from York (Toronto) overland to Lake Simcoe, by canoe to Georgian Bay and on to Manitoulin Island. After the gift-giving ceremony, the group continued canoeing along the northern shoreline of Lake Huron, through the straits past St. Joseph's Island, proceeding north into Lake Superior. Their return journey included a stop at Sault St. Marie, then continued south through the straits to Fort Mackinac, continuing on along the western shoreline of Lake Huron, and following the St. Clair River and Lake St. Clair to the Baldoon Settlement. From there the journey continued to Detroit, down the Detroit River to Amherstburg and Point Pelee. Leaving the lake, the party travelled overland by stagecoach past the Talbot Settlement, on to St. Thomas and London, following Dundas Street through to Brantford, Ancaster and Hamilton, and ultimately by train back to Toronto.

Beaches point and entered the main body of the lake,—ran 10 miles up Kempenfeldt Bay and called at Barrie; shores of this lake chiefly settled on by half pay Officers. At ___ past 5 entered a northern arm of the Lake called by the Indians Couchiching. Very beautiful wooded islands and very picturesque by indented shores. At the narrows at 6. Next across to see an Indian village building by Gov't. Slept on board the steamer.

21 July

Left the narrows in canoes 20 min. past 5 a.m. in 2 canoes. In about 2 hours got into the river Severn; breakfasted on a rock, got some excellent fish, immense numbers of water snakes; the river is extremely pretty, clear and very deep, 5 portages, some of the falls there are very picturesque. The 5th was very severe on the voyageurs, a mile and a ___ and very hot, mosquitoes in myriads. Jones lake is a fine piece of water but not a clearance or vestage of man nor for miles along the river except one Indian hut where we bought some potatoes planted among the stumps. Brought up for the evening on a little island where we hoped to have no mosquitoes but were sadly fooled and almost devoured. Pitched our tents, bathed and dined—The island covered with the calamitous weed[3] mentioned by Mrs. Jamieson and certainly 2 of our party suffered eyes brayed up. Sad objects! The voyageurs are most burly, lighthearted beings. After this longish portage, they start a song 'fall away as most....'

Monday 22 July

Up at ___ past 3 bathed. Struck tents and off at ___ past 4. 2 portages, breakfasted at 10 by a saw mill. Went to visit John

---

3 The weed referred to is poison ivy. Anna Jameson writes that they dined upon an island covered with "...a great quantity of a certain plant, which, if only touched, causes a dreadful eruption and ulcer all over the body." *Winter Studies and Summer Rambles in Canada*. (Toronto: MacClelland and Stewart, 1923) 433.

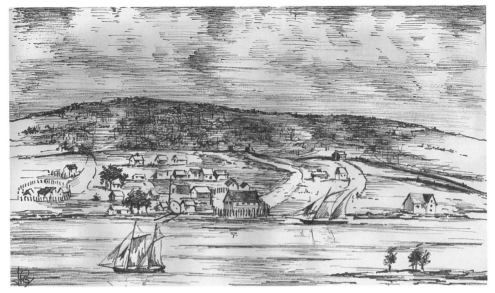

A view of Penetanguishene, 1818, taken from a picture in the John Ross Robertson Collection, showing the ship *Confiance*, and Magazine Island. *Courtesy the artist, F. R. Berchem.*

Aisance, an old Chippewa chief.[4] Received with military honours feu de jour—2 pagan Indians lately joined, painted looked very like cannibals—ran up to Cold water[5] and it really is named correctly as the instant you enter the river it becomes detectably cold. Met our heavy baggage and got 4 more canoes, reunited and paddled up to Penetanguishene;[6] stopped at the point where the barracks and store are and put up at Mrs. Wallaces very comfortable little Inn at 8 o'clock.

4. John Aisance was a chief of the Lake Simcoe Ojibwa. In 1830 Aisance and about 500 other natives were resettled at Coldwater. The resettlement was part of an experiment, under the direction of T. G. Anderson, Indian Agent, to civilize the natives. Peter S. Schmalz, *The Ojibwa of Southern Ontario.* (Toronto: University of Toronto Press, 1991) 144.

5 Coldwater was a small settlement on the Coldwater River, about halfway between Orillia and Penetanguishene. It was once an important link in the Great Lakes shipping and a port of call for the steamer *Gore*, the first Canadian owned steamship to ply the Great Lakes. Kenneth McNeill Wells, *Cruising the Georgian Bay.* (Toronto: Kingswood House, 1958) 68.

6 Penetanguishene was surveyed as early as 1811, but did not attract civilian settlers until troops and fur traders from Drummond Island were relocated there in the 1820s. Mary Ellen Perkins (comp.), *A Guide to Provincial Plaques in Ontario.* (Toronto: Natural Heritage/Natural History Inc., 1989) 247.

23 July

Went up the bay 3 miles to the village, Penetanguishene literally means "Look at the falling sand." What can the Toronto people mean by abusing it so much. In summer it seems to be delightful.[7] We got ice at the Inn here with our brandy and water lime juice. There are 3 stores, an Inn and about 50 houses. Walked home with Baker. Half way between the commuted pensioners are located in nice log houses, a garden behind each two sort of side streets. A church building here but no resident clergyman. Some of the half French Canadian and Indian women are really beautiful. Capt. Peabody (the only gentleman here) dined with us and had rather a jovial evening.

24 July

Hard rain which was much wanted and which we did not mind myself as we had very snug quarters at Mrs. Wallaces. Overhauled our fishing tackle.

25 July

[No Entry.]

26 July

The expedition set off at 10 a.m. in 6 canoes—beautiful morning but very hot. Left the bay. At the entrance is rather a curious bank no great height but very precipitous and apparently composed entirely of sand, whence the name of the place; kept a northerly course going up the Georgian Bay, through myriads of islands.[8]

7 Lieutenant Agnew appears to have been quite taken with the settlement at Penetanguishene. However, it appears that the close proximity of the settlement to a naval and military establishment had given the village a poor reputation. For more on the military and naval establishment there see, Elsie McLeod Jury, *The Establishments at Penetanguishene.* (London: University of Western Ontario, 1959).
8 Here Lieutenant Agnew is referring to the 30 000 Islands situated along the east coast of Georgian Bay.

The most remarkable lay upon our left soon after opening on the lake and is called the giants tomb[9] which a stretch of imagination may cause it to resemble. Stopped to dine at a 1/4 to 4 on a rocky island at ___ past seven brought up at a little flat stony islet where we pitched our camp; bathed, and an excellent supper—a very jovial evening.

27 July

Up at 4 and off at ___ past, rather heady for the early hours but the morning sun shook it off. Some of the passages through these numberless Islands is very beautiful. Stopped to breakfast at 8— about 12 passing Sable Island. larger than most of the rest. Lunch about 12. The thousands of passages among these clusters of Islands are of course to an unpracticed navigator as bad as the ancient labarinth, but the voyaguers and Indians kept the proper course with a wonderful correctness. They have certain marks, for instance, at one place an impression resembling a caraboo's foot on a rock though under water they look for in passing and farther a rock called the turtle is really an astonishing resemblance to a brobdingnag[10] head—they have a curious custom of leaving a present for the new comers and if an Indian have on arriving nothing to leave in return he will not take what was put before him. We found a small quid of tobacco and left a few shillings. Stopped at 7 on an island famous as having once been the slumbering place of Mrs Jameson and mentioned by her as resembling a Z. A strong breeze sprung up which kept off those torments the mosquitoes.

9   In native folklore, the island known as the Giant's Tomb is believed to be the resting place of Kitchikewana, a giant who long ago made the 30,000 Islands by throwing great chunks of granite into the water. The island has been described as his tomb, but another tradition suggests that Kitchikewana is just resting and will one day awake to once again throw rocks into Georgian Bay. Wells, *Cruising the Georgian Bay*, 55-56.
10   This term, meaning gigantic, refers to the inhabitants of the fabled region of Brobdingnag in Swift's *Gullivers's Travels*.

28 July

Dark morning but was pleasant. Started at 8. A breeze sprung up, made sail, kept rather clearer of the island [and] landed on a solid mass of rock at 1. Stopped at an island covered with gulls. Indians collected a good many eggs. Encamped at 7. The islands are very sterile in appearance, not a handful of soil by the 100 acres— though trees shoot thickly out of the crevices in the rocks.

29 July

Very dark morning but breeze fair enough to allow us to sail. Got in sight of the mainland and the fine outline of the La Cloche mountains loomed dimly on the horizon. At 10 we stopped to breakfast on an island as usual. Our little fleet scattered picturesque over the waters (I fortunately was on hand) now reflecting the dark clouds and a sea great and high enough to be beautiful beyond the green and woody shore and the towering mountains now distinctly defined and streaked with the light and shade as the sun beams struggled with the clouds. Was [,] I think the most beautiful scene I have yet beheld in Canada. Perhaps I ought to include the first peep of Quebec after passing Mont Morence.[11] Stopped a few minutes at a solitary house of a frenchman called Lamarondiere on the mainland, and very neat and nice it was. He traded occasionally with the Indians, giving them numerous little nuisances for furs.[12] Struck off nearly south, the great Manitoulin Island in view. Landed a few minutes at a settlement on the point nearest the mainland [and were] received with the usual salute; saw our schooner in the offing, paddled in and about half an hour after dark landed at the establishment.

11 Here Lieutenant Agnew is referring to Montmorency, which one passes as you approach Quebec City from the northeast up the St. Lawrence River.
12 Anna Jameson also mentions Lamorondiere, whom she describes as a fur trader "...living on the shore of a beautiful channel running between the mainland and a large island." *Winter Studies and Summer Rambles in Canada*, 424. Lieutenant Agnew's use of the term 'nuisances' when describing this trader's goods would suggest that he was taking advantage of the natives, offering them little for their furs.

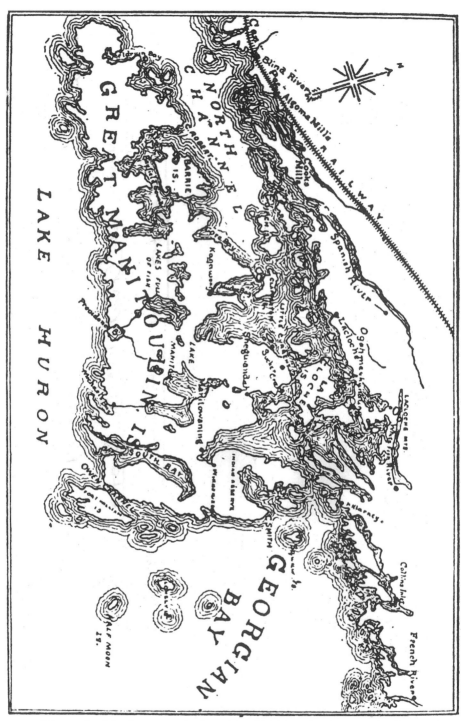

Manitoulin Island, circa 1895. From Harold Nelson Burden, *Manitoulin; or Five Years of Church Work Among Ojibwa Indians and Lumbermen. (1895).*

Tremendous *feu de jour* as we stepped from the canoe—about 1900 Indians were already assembled. A Capt. Anderson superintendant,[13] a Mr. Breff, English and Indian, reside here. The camp pitched on the sloping bank even very picturesque. Slept in a wigwam and eat[en] up by landflies.

30 July

Pitched our camp consisting of 2 [groups] of 3 tents and made ourselves very comfortable.

31 July

Crossed through the Indian camp—went three miles up the bay in canoes—I walked two miles and a half to an inland lake which is named Lake Jarvis. Col. Jarvis looked on a spot for a saw mill; which is to be erected instantly. Soil apparently very sick; shot 2 wild duck in a marshy pond. Had to pay a dollar to fetch them out.

1 August

Went 6 miles up the other side of the bay accompanied by the priest and walked about 3 miles to a very thriving Indian village. Several very nice fields of barley, potatoes, Indian corn and pumpkins. Very neat little chapel. Name of village Wequimicong; it lies on a bank sloping down to a very pretty little bay with a sandy beach.[14] The soil seemed excellent. The wild leak is in great abundance. The

13 Captain Thomas Gummersal Anderson apprenticed as a clerk in a Kingston shop before venturing into the Mississippi fur trade. In 1815 he accepted a position in the Indian Department and in 1836-37 played an important role in the development of Manitoulin Island as a native settlement and site of the annual gift-giving. Captain Anderson remained at Manitoulin until 1845, when he was promoted and moved to Toronto. Anderson remained in the service of the Indian Department until 1858. For more on the career of Captain Anderson see, Mrs. S. Rowe, "Anderson Record, From 1699-1896," *Ontario Historical Society, Papers and Records*. Vol. VI. Toronto: 1905. 116-132.

14 The present day spelling of this community is Wikwemikong. Native families began settling here around 1833 and by 1839 the settlements population had risen to about 350. In 1844 Jesuits took over the mission there and began instructing the inhabitants in agriculture, carpentry and various other trades. Shelley J. Pearen, *Exploring Manitoulin*. (Toronto, University of Toronto Press 1992) 6.

The above illustration is typical of descriptions of early Native settlements and closely follows that described by Lieutenant Agnew at Manitowawning. George Heriot, *Travels Through the Canadas*. London: 1807. *Archival and Special Collections, University of Guelph.*

original name of Manitoulin[15] is Towawmences and the settlements for Indians are at Manitowaning or "the City of Spirits."[16]

2 August

Hard rain but not withstanding the inclemency of the weather several Chippewa gave us a little exhibition of [their] dancing powers, crippling their persons which they can manage to make grotesque enough. Their dances are as stupid and lame as possible. The only music is an Indian drum, long and narrow, something like our tenor drum and a sort of monotonous howling accompanied by way of a song they keep time to regular laps in jumps sung as you may fancy a trained kangaroo leaning to and go round and

15 The word Manitoulin means 'Spirit Island', a name it received based on the native belief that it is the home of the Great Spirit, or Kitchi Manitou.
16 The village of Manitowaning developed as a direct result of the Treaty of 1836. The village was to be the centre of government and the Anglican mission from which the natives would be 'Europeanized' through instruction in agriculture and trades. In the Autumn of 1838, the village was "settled by a government party consisting of thirty-four persons, including Captain Anderson of the Indian Department, an Anglican clergyman, a doctor, a teacher, their families, as well as oarsmen and mechanics." For more on the early settlement of Manitowaning and Manitoulin Island see, Shelley J. Pearen. *Exploring Manitoulin*, 131.

Canoeing at Manitowawning. The above illustration was taken from the diary of Samuel Peter Jarvis (1842), the son of Samuel Peter Jarvis who was Indian Commissioner for Upper Canada. Lieutenant Agnew was travelling with both father and son during his tour to Manitoulin. The picture may well represent one of the canoe races held each year at the annual gift-giving. *Courtesy Hugh P. MacMillan.*

round now and then crowing like cocks or squealing like anything you please.[17] The day spent cleaning up. We announced a canoe race for one o'clock. Four canoes started, one entirely filled with squaws.[18] Race round a little island and back about 2 miles, betting was at first in favour of the ladies, but though they made an excellent start the fair ones rather swamped the bottom and came in a good third. Prize a gun, which was drawn for by the winning canoe. The next race was to be entirely for the fair, two canoes entered—

17 Lieutenant Agnew's negative view of Native dance and music is no doubt the result of his experience growing up in a society which adhered to a code of behaviour much more restrictive than that witnessed. Lieutenant Agnew was, as he so frequently points out, raised to be a gentleman, and such behaviour would have easily shocked Victorian sensibilities which demanded a high level of decorum and civility, and did not allow for any deviation from their narrow perspective.

18 The word 'squaw' has a Cree origin. The word implies that the woman is the container for the Spirit World to be born again into the physical world, and is a term representing the beauty of the woman. Regrettably, with the arrival of European colonizers, the original Cree word became corrupted to squaw with all the negative connotations of the times. Conversation with Sandra Laronde, Native Women in the Arts, summer 1999.

only to the Island gather and willow like the maid of the Inn and back, distance probably about a mile and a quarter. An excellent race and our old friends of the last race won by about 2 lengths and got a glorious brass kettle for a prize, a great object to have as it is an invaluable article in preparing maple syrup.[19]

3 August

Puttered about the camp and made a few purchases of mats and other Indian curiosities by the help of a few Indians words and signs and mixed French and English, beginning to get on very well; the chief spectacles in the camp are an eagle, a heron, a young bear and beaver. The latter [I] was very anxious to buy— but the owners would not part with for any money. Rather a romantic as well as a scaly tale (tail!!!) attaches itself to it. The lady of the wigwam, who lost her child last autumn and having found this little beaver this spring, has adopted it as a child and does look upon it as such. It is a curious little thing none larger than a muscrat; webbed feet and very like a wild duck and a very peculiar tale the exterior of the substance of a wall. It feeds on bark and biscuit. Its cry is quite like an infant.

4 August

Attended the Established Church in the forenoon. The service is read in Indian as well as the sermon. There were probably about 150 Indians present. 2 men even baptised. In the afternoon we attended Church in English about a dozen besides ourselves composed the congregation. I had rather a touch of the passibles[20] but stood by bull dogs ___ ___.

19 In *Winter Studies and Summer Rambles in Canada*, Anna Jameson describes a similar day of canoe races, the women taking part, at the Manitoulin gift-giving. 406-407.
20 Passible means "Capable of feeling or suffering; susceptable of impressions from external agents." Therefore, it would seem that Lieutenant Agnew was greatly moved by the church service and fought to control his emotions. However, his use of the phrase "stood by bulldogs" might imply that he was physically unwell.

By the 1830s, the process of 'civilization' had progressed to the point that Native dress had been heavily influenced by European styles. Lieutenant Agnew, Anna Jameson and other contemporary commentators noted the variety and mix of Aboriginal clothing. This illustration was taken from George Heriot, *Travels Through the Canadas*. London: 1807. *Archival and Special Collections, University of Guelph.*

5 August

Had several matches at rifle shooting. Tomahawkes and pipes as the end prizes. Excellent practice. And in the afternoon a match in canoes round the island, Indians against the Canadians. Notwithstanding our Canadian friends being perfectly confident in their own powers the red men won. At a caution we made up a prize of 6 dollars for them and they left the ground quite cock an hoof. Our Canadians got up a dance in the evening which we looked in upon, the attendance of ladies was not numerous and it was kept up till the light going out gave them a hint. Hard gales, almost a hurricane in the night and thunderstorms.

6 August

Fine. Bottled off a cask of sherry.

7 August

Fine morning. At 2 presents were given out to the chiefs and warriors, they sat in rows on the bank, leaning about military double
distance between each in the most perfect order, the Chiefs taking
the right of the front row. They each get a piece of cloth and calico, a blanket, butcher knife, awls, toothcombs and the chiefs a
shawl. They also have given out in the camp needles and thread,
flints, powder and shot,—they sit as patiently as possible till told
to dispense and then off they go crowing and hooping as merry
and good humoured as possible.[21] When would you find the same
number of white men as orderly? The nations assembled were
Chippewa's, Ottawa's and Potawatomi's.[22] The numbers even as
nearly as possible. Chiefs 40, warrior chiefs 37, inferior chiefs 14,
warriors (including every man and ___) 782, wives of chiefs and
warrior chiefs 55, women 959.

8 August

Bought a very handsome head dress made of a raven with an
eagle's plume and moose hair taken from the head of a Chippewa. Tremendous thunderstorm and rain to match in the night.
Today presents were distributed to the women and children com-
mencing at 12 o'clock. The ladies sat in the same order as the men
all afternoon. The better halves of the chiefs taking the right of the
front line, although the motley group did answer the expectations
of those who look for the beauty supposed to belong to the majestic uncontaminated descendants of the ancient lords and ladies of
the Lakes, still amongst them a few really pretty girls and women
might be seen smilingly receiving their present and showing their

21 Again, Agnew's language reveals the paternalistic and Eurocentric views of
his culture and time.
22 Historically all three of the aboriginal groups mentioned were native to the
Lake Huron region, including the northern shore of Lake Huron, the Bruce
Peninsula and northern Michigan. From about the 1780s, many of these Native
groups signed agreements which saw them relinquish much of their lands and
settle on reserves. R. Cole Harris (ed.), *Historical Atlas of Canada: From Beginning
to 1800*. (Toronto: University of Toronto Press, 1987) Plate 18.

pretty teeth in great perfection. Their eyes are very beautiful, but with very few exceptions you might really think they had all an attack of hydrophobia from the wonderful objections they have to contaminate their skins with the water of the lake—which God knows is cheap enough. Here and there a more delicate fair one would hold a very gay fringed parasol over her to shelter her pretty little visage from the sun.[23] Whilst a few less civilized Chippewa's, despising their effeminate tendency sat out with their bare arms and sides—a strip of cloth something like braes holding a covering for their breasts and back—they each got a blanket, shroud for petticoats, fine cloth for leggings; calico for a shirt, and here I gained a little popularity by picking out some dozen or two of the prettiest patterns and exchanging them for more sombre and with a few more favoured by nature (and myself) had marked in a tour of inspection and as far as pretty and beaming eyes turned upon my happy self I was amply rewarded. They also get a knife, awl, comb and needle. It was past seven before we had finished the whole. Hard rain in the night.

9 August

The total number besides those mentioned on the 7th was:
Boys 10 to 15–209, 5 to 10–204, 1 to 4–217
Girls 10 to 14–181, 5 to 9–146, 1 to 4–248
Today the men were assembled and had three or four pound of shot each distributed among them and some bullets and flints. They then were started off to a little Island to have powder divided among them for fear of accident and it was a beautiful sight to see a hundred or two canoes immediately flying along the water towards the place of division. Nothing can be more orderly than the manner in which they divide all those things among themselves. They also got each a good bundle of pigtails. [Entertained] the natives by letting off a few sky rockets and blue lights in the wood.

23 In the summer of 1839, Lieutenant Agnew was 21 years of age, seemingly with an eye for the ladies.

10 August

Grand council on for the occasion and found the chiefs assembled in the place used for the chapel. Behind them as many of the warriors (probably about 100) as could find room took their places. Opened by a short prayer from Mr. Brough,[24] then Colonel Jarvis[25] made an address to them. Siginauk,[26] principal chief of the Chippewa's and interpreter standing behind and translating sentence by sentence which made it rather a tedious affair; then several of the chiefs rose and spoke, their speech being translated in the same manner. The calumet[27] and a very handsome one it was, was then placed on our table and presented to Colonel Jarvis and we all took our parts in the ceremony by taking a puff or two at it; Colonel Jarvis then dismissed the council, refusing all those who made any requests of him for answers till the next day between services. I was rather fortunate in buying a pipe from one of the Chippewa (Kimiwan)[28] a very fine fellow whose name has been handed down to posterity by Mrs. Jameson as one of the flowers of the flock. In the evening a considerable number

24 The Reverend Charles Crosbie Brough, (b. Carlow, Ireland, 1794) the Church of England minister appointed to undertake the mission on Manitoulin Island in 1838. See, Rendall M. Lewis. "The Manitoulin Letters of the Rev. Charles Crosbie Brough," *Ontario History*. Vol. XLVIII. No. 2. 1956.

25 Colonel Jarvis (1790-1857), the Commissioner responsible for the relations with the Native People on Manitoulin Island and the surrounding area. In 1842, he was involved in a controversial legal action when the Government and an Ojibway Chief brought charges against him. He was accused of committing a crime against a Native girl while crossing Lake Simcoe by steamer. In the end, he was acquitted.

26 Shiginauk (Singauk), was a member of the Odawa Indians who lived between the years 1768 and 1866. He fought for the British side in the War of 1812 and served as an interpreter for the British garrison on Drummond Island (between Manitoulin Island and Sault Ste. Marie). In 1832, he settled in what is now known as Coldwater, bringing his people with him. In 1839, when in his late sixties, he moved to Manitoulin Island where he stayed for the remainder of his life. For more information see: Donald Smith, *Sacred Feathers*. Toronto: University of Toronto Press, 1987.

27 The North American Native pipe of peace, the smoking of which was a pledge of good faith.

28 Kimiwan (Jameson's spelling is Kim, e, wun) was a chief of the Ottawas. Jameson met him while visiting the Schoolcrafts in Michigan. She relates that, "He now stood before me, one of the noblest figures I ever beheld, above six feet high, erect as a forest pine." Anna Jameson, *Winter Studies and Summer Rambles*. (facsimile reproduction) (Toronto: Coles Publishing Co., 1972) 53–54.

of guns, tomahawks, kettles and tin cans were distributed to successful applicants.

Sunday 11 August

Packed up and made all ready for a start. Two thirds of the Indian wigwams were now gone, and the owners houses and all. Many miles across off the lake, the poor island began to look indeed deserted and following the rest of the red skin fashionably we said good bye to the Manitowaning at four p.m., our establishment reduced to 4 canoes. We proceeded in a westerly course leaving Heywood Sound[29]—the shores become much higher and rich, beautiful foliage down to the water's edge added much to its beauty; in an hour or two the setting sun throwing a beautiful light on the now finely shaped ___ of the Island. Was very picturesque and running on till 8, we stopped at a small Indian village about 12 miles from our starting place and encamped for the night.

12 August

Up at ___ after 5. Beautiful morning. Stopped at 8 on a small island for breakfast; we now had the Cloche range on our right. The varying light and shadow on these fine mountains, a constant variety of outline, added much to the pleasure of our voyage. At about 2 we arrived at an establishment of the Hudson Bay Company; at the foot of the mountains the cliffs above, which are of white marble, look very much like the chalk on many of the English roads. Mr. Anderson belonging to the Canadians produced some very excellent Madiera and port to which, for fear he would think us particular, we did ample justice. Beautiful nuts were growing wild

---

29 Heywood Sound was the name given to present day Manitowaning Bay by Captain Henry Wolsey Bayfield (1795-1885), who surveyed the region in the 1820s. Bayfield was a naval officer and self-taught nautical surveyor who mapped lakes Erie, Huron and Superior. He also charted the coasts of Prince Edward Island, Nova Scotia and the St. Lawrence River. Mary Ellen Perkins (comp.), *A Guide to Provincial Plaques in Ontario*, (Toronto: Natural Heritage, 1989) 247.

Capt. Thomas G. Anderson, Indian Agent. Andrew Agnew meets Thomas Anderson on Manitoulin, and refers to him in the journal entry dated August 12. From Mrs. S. Rowe, "Anderson Record, From 1699-1896," *Ontario Historical Society, Papers and Records*. Vol. VI. Toronto: 1905.

in great abundance; passed a beautiful cap called Point Wade Channel covered with oak trees; stopped about 7; the greatest no. of blueberries and largest I ever saw growing on the rocks.

13 August

Off at 6. One of our boats fell in with a bear swimming from an island to the main; pestered his way by firing four balls at him and took effect, but he unfortunately made shore. We landed on the Chippewa hunting country and gave chase but he gave us the artful dodge and made off.[30] Breakfasted at 12 on the serpents, so called for a number of figures cut out in the thick moss by Indians on the rocks. Blew rather hard and a little accident happened to one of our canoes which made us put in for an hour. Shot several brace of pigeons. Gathered quantities of wild cherries, nuts and gooseberries. Stopped at Mississaglene (literal meaning the several mouths of a river) a very pretty little place. Saw a number of ducks and pigeons. An establishment of the Hudson Bay Company. The river is very pretty. The settlement about 2 miles up. We took up our___ at the house of a half breed who kindly gave us up his apartment—like the cottars "who lived in a stable"—after an excellent dinner and sufficient libations to the rosy God we all stretched our buffalo skins on the floor and courted balmy repose!!!!!

14 August

Excellent new milk being discovered we refreshed the inner man with a drink and off at 7. Breakfasted on an island at ___ past 9—passed Snake Island—intensely hot. Made for St. Joseph's and arrived at ___ past 8. Got into a Mr. Pack's house, who was fortunately at the Sault, and made ourselves very comfortable. At this place where we stopped there was probably about 80 houses and 20 acres of cleared land, a wind mill and a store; the fort is about 8 mile round; on the island there is nearly 80,000 acres of land and 45,000 considered good land if cleared.

15 August

Left Joseph's at ___ past 8. Rainy before noon. Came up at Bears

30 In a letter to his father describing this chase, Lieutenant Agnew blamed the escape of "Master Bruin" to the cowardice of the Canadians who "...would not paddle close to him. We could easily have finished him, but they in a most disgraceful manner allowed him to weather us and gain the shore..." Letter dated 25th, September 1839. Edinburgh. Scottish Record Office. GD 154/745/11 (14). Such a comment suggests that Lieutenant Agnew had little experience with bears, the Canadians being well aware of the threat offered by getting too close.

The Rev. Dr. O'Meara was instrumental to the establishment of the settlement at Manitowaning. When construction of the settlement's Anglican church was underway, the Rev. Dr. O'Meara journeyed to England to raise the funds needed for its completion. He was successful. From William Munro, *Manitoulin Echoes, From Bluff, Dale, Lake and Stream.* Gore Bay: 1900. *Special Collections, University of Guelph.*

Point at ___ past 12. Cleared up in the afternoon. Steamer the Gov. Marcy passed us going up to the Sault. Entered the river at a little before seven. Stiff wind to full against; distinctly heard the Sault[31]—owing to a slight smash to one canoe did not arrive until 9. Took up our quarters in the mission house—a large and very comfortable building, almost unfurnished which however suited our looks famously; every civility from a Mr. Lampson a young divinity student in posession in the [care] of the Rev. Mr. O Meara.[32]

16 August

Beautiful morning. Immediately after breakfast started with

31 Here he is referring to the roar of the rapids, which could be heard from a considerable distance.
32 The Reverend O'Meara was minister at Sault St. Marie, and later at the settlement of Manitowaning on Manitoulin Island. With the aid of one of the Natives, Reverend O'Meara translated the services, New Testament and part of the Old Testament into Ojibway. Harold Nelson Burden, *Manitoulin; or Five Years of Church Work Among Ojibway Indians and Lumbermen.* (London: Simpkin, Marshall, Hamilton & Kent, 1895) 27.

Working a Canoe up a Rapid. W. H. Bartlett in Willis' *Canadian Scenery*. Volume II. 1848. *Special Collections, University of Guelph.*

Lindsay in a canoe with two Indians for the Sault St. Marie. The mastery the Indians have of their canoe exceeds all telling. They paddle up until in the immediate influence of the rapids they guide their little canoe with 2 long poles; the graceful art with which they handle these is indeed a study for a painter. At the strongest parts of the current they push their punts along with the most unerring certainty, passing between rocks not 5 feet apart through which the water is going to an inexperienced eye with considerable force and which a little mistake or slip would cause instant destruction.

Even in the very midst of the boiling rapid they once were perfectly still for a quarter of an hour, sitting at each end apparently carelessly holding their poles in the water with most perfect ease; they carry a long fish spear and scoop (a gigantic landing net with a handle some 14 feet long) in the boat and use either of these as occasion may require with wonderful dexterity; they not only net but spear their fish or scoop them out in the strongest currents, an attempt not only impractible to any one else but even to see them was more than any of ourselves could manage; we went up the English side and up two smaller rapids encircling two beautiful little islands. The foliage hanging over the water and numbers of King fishers hovering over the stream. Then crossing above to near the American shore we shot the main rapid with surprising velocity and at the same time almost unperceptable motion. Then turned the head of the canoe as easily as if they were in a mill pond our almost magical boatmen crossed slanting the boiling waters broad side on; the sensation is more exciting than can be imagined; and sitting as comfortable as in an easy chair in your graceful canoe within the midst of this turmoil of waters, above and below water the bright blue waters still and mirror like reflecting all the thousand tents of the brushy wood upon its banks, on each side vessels on hand and laying as steady as in Ramsgate harbour.[33] Upon their bosoms beyond little evergreen isles; and the mountains enclosing Lake Superior in the background; the whole is almost too intoxicating to admire sufficiently—why is this lovely spot so little heard of? We afterwards went to Fort Brady, the American village; nothing can be pleasanter than the alteration [deportment?] of the natives. If all Yankees were as well behaved we should have a very different state of affairs upon the frontier.[34] The fort is enclosed with slight stockade work; there are 70 men, and very different from the general account of Yankee soldiers; really very clean and smart; the best store is at the southend inside the fort [where] there are three other very good stores, a billiard room and a tailors shop. Delighted with whole days amusements; I often think now with Virgil "Hic ___ ___ ___ gravabit" No end of stories for the Old Country fireside!!! Music and old Manitoulin amusements in the evening.

33 This is likely a reference to the busy harbour at Ramsgate in Kent, England.
34 It would seem that Agnew is most positive towards the overall conduct of the Native members of the group. In his opinion they rate more positively than the Yankees.

17 August

Beautiful day—Went out with the Colonel in a canoe to the Sault, much the same country as yesterday; but a great addition to the scene in a beautiful Osprey hovering over the water and occasional darting into the current for its scaly prey then shaking his wings and up till almost out of sight. Speared 2 fine Pickerel. The American Officers kindly sent us several joints of beef and a large quantity of ice, both very acceptable. Crossed to the other side, very lucky in getting a watch glass. Puttered about with my gun and bathed in the river. The Colonel and Meads caught 6 dozen fine trout and Colonel Jarvis shot 6 ___ brace wild duck. Buchanan and Lindsay went 7 miles down the river invigorated.

Sunday 18 August

Buchanan and Lindsay came back only 5 ___ brace. Attended service read by Mr. Sampson. Very hot. The Church is situated on the hill behind the mission house about 1/4 or ___ a mile from the Sault. There are ships up the lake and the ___ ___ of the Sault the rest of the river and a large tract of the Michigan state is very well worth the walk which is not ___ on the hottest day. Bathed in the afternoon.

19 August

Another splendid day. We were rather interested this morning by the appearance of one of the wild Chippewa's who had attracted our interest, particularly at the Manitowaning, by his fine bearing and address. He was now altered in every way crestfallen and hardly able to rise his gaze from the ground, his face painted black, which is by way of mourning among the Indians. He had just received accounts of members of his tribe having been surprised by their deadly enemies the Sioux, and three villages massacred, of his own nothing remained, every relation, friend and chief had

Hudson's Bay Company Fur Trading Post at Sault Ste. Marie. The Hudson's Bay Company took possession of the fort at Sault Ste. Marie in 1821 and maintained the site in order to prevent its rival, the American Fur Company, from monopolizing the fur trade of the area. *Courtesy Sault Ste. Marie Public Library.*

fallen by these ruthless ___. He came to ask for guns. Hardly any remained but Col. Jarvis gave him 3 tomahawks and one gun, which he thankfully received. He is now away to the far west and woe betide the luckless Sioux that may come within his grip. Different parties made up for shooting and fishing. No difficulty here in killing time. Lounged about the portage and lesser rapid with ___. I looked in on Mr. Nowse of the Hudson Bay Company where I regaled the body with some excellent port and the mind with some [tales] of late Mr. Banks tour. The game begs ___ for the day. ___ 14 dozen brace of ducks and some fish.

Tuesday 20 August

Today I may consider certainly as an era in my life having paid

my first and I fear my last visit to that Lake of Lakes[,] L. Superior. One peep at its finely watered and beautiful indented
shores. One glance from the exaggeration of the gros cap at the
bright and unmuffled bosom of this inland ocean. One plunges
into its pure and bouquet water. Clear, clearer than the crystal
or almost the air itself. And now I am back again at the beautiful Sault St. Marie which I must bid adeiu to tomorrow, and
to it too probably for ever. To think of to picture ever and again
to the minds eye the gigantic wonders of the far west!!! Lindsay, another young friend and myself started this morning at a
1/4 before 7 for the Gros Cap which (although a long reach
below bears the name of Lake Superior) is first at the entrance
of the bona fide Lake. We had a fine ___ morning. Crossed the
portage, having sent on a fresh canoe to thwart delay and stopping half an hour or so for breakfast. Brought up at the Gros
Cap 1/4 after 11. The main body of the lake here comes in near
to the right on rounding the point. To the left the American
shore stretched away to the west with a little ___. The Yankee
side is high opposite our cape, well wooded and prettily ideal
little creeks extend till all becomes hazy in the ___ on our own
shore. The Gros Cap rears its craggy head darkly towering over
the sympathizing ___ it is almost perpendicular 240 feet in
height with fine pines and firs at the top and thick Hazel bush-
es and maple at the bottom. Cut off its bold rock sides an Indian path leads up to the top which we of course lost no time in
scrambling up. It is very steep, and hands had to do their duty
as well as feet in the ascent in accomplishing which we were
much indebted to the friendly trees as a suffiet and was amply
rewarded by the magnificent view. Any future traveller who
pursues our route may have the satisfaction of reading my
humble name upon a pine near the top. Coming down again
was rather slippery work and we eased the thing to ourselves
on arriving at the bottom by a most delicious bath, the clean-
ness of the waters almost exceeds belief. I think it something

particularly pleasant in a draught of them. Although prudence being the better part of valour we generally took the precaution of qualifying them with a little *Eau de vie* by way of poisoning the air ___. We returned much delighted with our days excursion; and shot the rapids. Rather a nervous affair as our voyageurs, although skillful to a degree, had never gone down them before, however we are all safe with an excellent appetite for dinner. As the sun was setting I walked up the hill to the Church to take a farewell view of the Sault which was looking more beautiful than ever. On my return I found Col. Spark just coming in with 42 lb. of Trout, no bad days sport. In the evening Chinguacoose[35] (the Young Pine) the chief of the settlement paid us a visit accompanied by his interpreter and 2 sons. He sat down and had a long ___ over his glass of grog and a pipe. Lindsay exhibited several feats of cunning which astonished the old gentleman exceedingly; and he stayed to a late hour highly delighted with us all.[36]

Wednesday 21 August

Left with much regret the Sault St. Marie at ___ past nine this morning down the river and proceeding south took a channel to the westward of our course up. Touched at ___ past three at a point called the sailors camp. Passing George lake and Sugar

35 Anna Jameson describes Chinguacoose [Shinguaconse] as being "not an hereditary chief, but an elective or war-chief, and owes his dignity to his bravery and to his eloquence..." Shinguaconse played an important role in the War of 1812, was at Fort Malden and the battle of the Moravian towns. *Winter Studies and Summer Rambles*, 375. Chief Shingwaukonse, or "Little Pine", respected member of the Medewinwin, lived between the years 1790 and 1854. He was leader, for over twenty-five years, of the Garden River Ojibwa, who occupied a territory spanning from Garden River, Ontario east to Batchewana Bay. By following ancient Ojibwa traditional leadership principles of compromise, resistance and adaptation, he became a successful political leader, establishing links with Upper Canadian government agencies while preserving Native religion, culture and values. For more information, see: Janet E. Chute, *The Legacy of Shingwaukonse: A Century of Native Leadership*. Toronto: University of Toronto Press, 1998.

36 Between the lines the author has written the phrase "copper into gold" suggesting that Lindsay was performing some slight of hand tricks for entertainment.

Island. Beautiful moonlight night with waters as smooth as glass. Arrived at a small clearance belonging to Major Rains in at St. Joseph's Island and encamped at ___ past 9.

22 August

Up at daylight, a cup of coffee and off at 5. One of the most beautiful rainbows I ever saw. A complete arch and very vividly coloured, a second bow rising from the principal one at an angle of about 20 degrees. Ominous however of rain which soon followed and lasted several hours. Coasted the Mainland Michigan state,—and landed on it for breakfast at 9. A bath. Kept the same course to an island opposite Mackinaw going merrily along before a fresh breeze and here we left an Indian of our party who could not face the natives, a brother of his having murdered a son of Col. Boyds many years before. A stormy evening. Made a traverse of 12 miles and a half and arrived at the fine island of Mackinaw at ___ past 7. Encamped near the Church although a Mr. Lochcroft kindly offered to do his best ___ all or ___ .

23 August

Mackinaw is a beautiful island standing high out of the Lake the crags picturesquely covered with wood—about 9 miles in circumference. It is one of the oldest settlements in the Canadas having been 'colonised' by the French in 1680—it is naturally a very strong position and the fort if properly defended would be almost impregnable. It afterwards came into our hands and was surrendered to the Yankees in 1789. We again took it by surprise in 1813 and it was most absurdly again given up to brother Jonathan by our dunderheaded commissioner in 1818. It is a very important position being situated in the straits of Michilimakinack and a complete key to the lakes. There are 2 churches with little tin cupolas which add much to the civilness of this new town. Two or three excellent gentlemen's houses, 6 or 8 excellent 'stores' besides several smaller ones and the great convenience of at least one steam-er a day calling. There are at present at least 100 Indian wigwams on the beach who have come here to receive their annuities in lieu of lands they had given up to the American government. After breakfast we called on Mr. J.[H.]Schoolcraft Indian Agent.[37] He lives in an excellent house. Mrs. Schoolcraft [is] half Indian and a very pleasing person she is so much animation of countenance great self possession [and] at the same time perfectly feminine, her eyes when in conversation light up beautifully so much richness and vivacity in their disposition. Her voice is extremely pleasing. We found the 2 Yankee officers here who really were very gentle-manly looking young men. We afterwards visited the fort. You ascend a flight of steps looking at the hill, below which the town is situated—though strongly situated the walls are very crumbly—and the Old fort which is very much higher has been blown up. A fine view commanding an immense strait from the top. We afterwards took a tour around the town. I made some pur-chases and then visited Mr. Schoolcraft (of Jamesonian notori-ety)[38] an elder sister of Mr. J.[H.]S.[,] Mrs S. was away[,] but she was delighted to see us. Though perhaps her sister [in-law] has the advantage in personal appearance she has quite as pleasing a manner and address and if may cozen an opinion on so short an acquaintance I'd say she was if not more talented at least deeper read. I have seldom met a person in whom I felt more interested in a morning call. Had a very interesting little conversation on Indian antiquities. Afterwards adjoined to her garden. In front of the house an apple orchard where we ___ upon her currants in a ___. I afterwards walked to a great natural curiosity, an immense arch—formed out of the limestone rock you come suddenly upon

37 Henry Rowe Schoolcraft, born in Albany County in 1793, became a cele-brated author and ethnologist. In 1822 he was appointed Agent for Indian Affairs on the Northwest Frontiers and in 1823 he married Jane Johnston, eldest daughter of Sir John Johnston. Following her death in the early 1840s, he moved to New York City and was a co-founder of the American Ethnological Society.
38 Anna Jameson spent some time with the Schoolcrafts while travelling through Michigan and was extremely taken with Mrs. Schoolcraft. Lieutenant Agnew's frequent reference to Anna Jameson's work suggests that it had a con-siderable impact upon him and was extremely popular at the time as he seems to imply that it was a work with which most people would be familiar.

Henry Rowe Schoolcraft, both an Indian Agent and noted ethnologist, was an important figure in colonial Michigan. He was a prolific writer who, in 1851, wrote an interesting work detailing his time spent among Michigan's Native Peoples. The above illustration is from his work, *Thirty Years with the Indian Tribes*. (1851). *Courtesy Michigan State Archives.*

it. It is situated at the bottom of a slope and rises I should say at least 150 feet from the sea; it is the most perfect model, (if I may call model a door this majestic) of a gothic ruin possible and looking on the mighty lake rolling its billows to its feet, and quantities of fine wild wood above and below it. A grander spectacle you can hardly find any where. It is impossible to detach from the imagination this idea of the lake being the ocean itself. I afterwards took a long ramble in the island though then in some panic I only saw a squirrel and 'a snake'—but beautiful trout are caught all round; filberts and wild raspberries are everywhere with greatest numerance. In the evening the steamer Jefferson[39] from Chicago on her way to Detroit touched here. I went on board. She is an immense boat—quite a day with fore turns of the deck. A number of passengers and some very pretty girls were standing by some flowers by the ladies cabin. We had a thunderstorm and heavy rain all night, which our tents did not protect us from as much as we might have wished.

24 August

Cleared up about 10. In morning strolled about the woods which here are open and pleasant to walk through; dark a long time by the glorious arch; we were fortunate enough to find a store supplied with Dublin porter, rather an incredible treat and did justice to it accordingly. I afterwards started along the shore under the cliffs and bathed, and afterwards went to a curious small natural cave, famous as the hiding place of Henry[40] an old traveller who was hid here by a friendly Indian after the general massacre of the whites some 150 years ago. Him the savages too used to their feasts and the ___ [bones are] very numerous although now they have nearly all been conveyed ___ as ___ of course I ___ one or two crumbling fragments as a part of the ceremony.[41] The Great Western, a splendid steamer for Chicago and the

39 The *Thomas Jefferson*, a steamer of 428 tons built in 1835. "Sketches of the Long Ago," *Michigan Historical Collections*. Vol. 14. 543.
40 Alexander Henry (1739-1824), a fur trader of some repute who published (1807) an interesting and lively account of his years spent in the fur trade. See *Travels and Adventures In Canada and the Indian Territories*. James Bain (ed.) (Rutlands, Vermont: C.E. Tuttle Co., 1969).
41 Henry was secreted away to a cave by his native friend Wawatam in order to protect him during an evening of drunken revelry. Upon waking, Henry was shocked to find that he had slept the night among a heap of human bones, what he believed to be the remnants of past prisoners sacrificed and devoured at war feasts. Henry, *Travels and Adventures*. 105-110.

View of Fort Mackinac, circa 1842. The fort was established in 1780 when the British moved the old French garrison to the more strategic island location. Once of great military importance, the fort is now regularly invaded by thousands of tourists enjoying the scenery and history offered by the region. *Illustration courtesy of Michigan State Archives.*

Rochester[42] with a Lady of pleasure for the Sault called in the evening—beautiful moonlight night.

Sunday 25 August

Up at ___ past 5 and off at 7. Our Indian crew were beastly drunk and rather ___. Stopped at 10 and breakfasted on Bois Blanc Island. It is partially cleared on one side and about 36 miles round. After breakfast crossed to the main (territory of Michigan) ___ past 2 stopping once or twice we coasted along, there the Straits of Michilimackinack course east and at 6 brought up at a glorious camping ground.

42 The *Great Western*, an impressive steamer of 781 tons completed in the summer of 1839, and the *Rochester*, a 400 ton vessel built in 1838, were both excellent examples of the burgeoning Great Lakes shipbuilding trade. Such ships were an important link in the development of the newly-settled regions to the west. "Sketches of Long Ago," *Michigan Historical Collections*. V.14. 543.

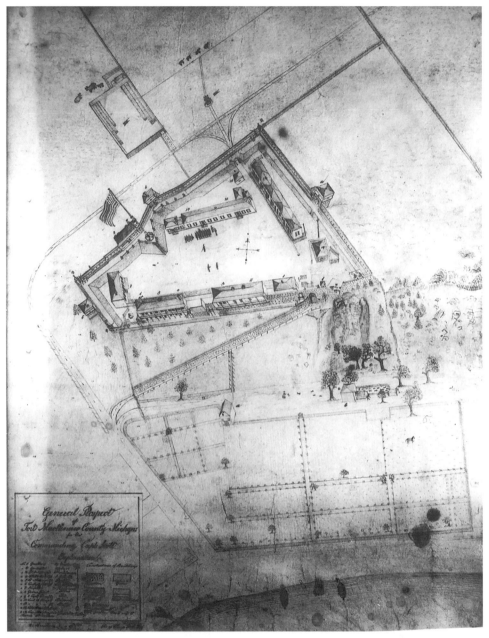

Michilimackinac (Fort Mackinaw). This illustration was drawn by Captain S. Eastman, U.S.A. and represents the fort as it appeared about 1850. *Courtesy Michigan State Archives.*

26 August

Rather a stormy night but our tents were true to their duty and did not give in. Too high a sea in the morning to make a start, which I did not at all regret as I gained a good snooze and a gentlemanly breakfast at 10. However, it cleared up famously and soon after 12 we launched our canoes. The boating and getting in was rather a dicey operation in the surf, fresh breeze, and many heavy squalls ___ as much as we could we put the best face on the matter and bounded away over a tumultuous Lake. No accident however as we let fly once or twice when a heavy gust struck us and we chose an excellent camping ground at ___ past 5 after managing nearly 40 miles—coming on to ___.

27 August

Wind coninuing to increase in the night and a heavy swell in the morning. No possibility of moving—so we ranged along the beach and through the woods with our guns. I only fell in with a few beautiful lake Chatterns[43] which I shot as ___. Saw an eagle or two at a distance, but the tremendous storm kept most living things in the depth of the woods. Found a ___ ___ and took some ___ out as relics. The Colonel was very unwell and had to turn in. Beautiful night but hard gale.

28 August

Lovely morning and the sea quite down. Rather chilly, however put into Rest Isle[44] and breakfast at ___ past 10. Observed a small settlement. Fair breeze, ran gloriously on before it. At 3 came in sight of a lighthouse on Thunder Island. At ___ past four ran in between the Island and the main. Saw 3 Yankee schooners lying at anchor in lea of the Island; the Colonel became so unwell we put in and pitched our tents.

---

43 It is unclear what type of bird he is referring to here, although it is possibly the Common Tern, a water bird similar to a gull and indigenous to the Great Lakes region.
44 This would be Presque Isle.

29 August

Brilliant morning. The Colonel much better. Crossed Thunder Bay in about 4 hours. Wind shifted more to the east—a heavy sea rising. Stopped at ___ past 6 at River Au Sable, found a schooner and a number of Yankees on a fishing and hunting expedition. Saw hundreds of ducks. 110 miles from Fort Gratiot.[45]

30 August

Bagged about a dozen ducks before breakfast not to be despised as our larder is getting low, off at ___ past 9. Went 5 miles to point Au Sable, and then ran about 10 miles up Saginaw bay. A good breeze but rather too much easterly which obliged us to be rather close hauled for canoe sailing, crossed 10 miles of the bay to Traverse Island[46] when the wind freshening we stopped about 3. It is a beautiful little Island about 3 miles round, well clothed with wood but pleasant to walk in. Ground very prettily broken and oak copses prettily grouped about and here and there the wild fir clustering over them forms beautiful studies for sketches. There is a pretty little lake in it and we proved fatal to some 6 brace of pigeons, a duck and a variety of robins, woodpeckers and so on. The best whortleberries[47] I ever met with.

31 August

Beautiful morning. Stayed all day roaming about this 'little Isle of beauty'; dined at 5, and at 6 embarked. Made our traverse of 8 miles to the main and travelled all night. A course which I cannot however recommend to my friends—fortunately we had the comfort of a fine moonlight night, and still, ___ the strangest expression as I was disputed.

45 Fort Gratiot is located above modern day Port Huron at the mouth of the St. Clair River.
46 Probably Charity Island, which is situated about halfway across Saginaw Bay of Lake Michigan.
47 Whortleberry is another name for the Black Huckleberry, a shrub common to the Great Lakes region which produces tangy and sweet black berries from July to September.

Sunday 1 September

Lovely morning. Stopped at 9 to breakfast and bathed which was very refreshing after the nights work. Soon afterwards found a fishing establishment in a creek and further on a saw mill where we replenished our larder with some excellent potatoes (60 miles from Fort Gratiot) and some young Indian corn. An excellent ingredient in pea soup. The shore became more picturesque as before they were very flat and uninteresting. Put in and bought some venison from some Indians. They had just killed an Elk (the Wapiti deer) the horns, the finest I ever saw, which one of our party immediately secured. Stopped at ___ past 6. Glorious dinner of pea soup (a ham bone in it!!!) with the young Indian corn, venison hash, stewed pigeon and young potatoes—a dinner for the grand mogul. We allowed ourselves an extra bottle on the strength of it and determined to immortalize the memory of it by naming the point. Only dispute which may cause a variance to our charts was between 'Good Dine Point' or 'Cape Blow Out'.

2 September

Fine again, off at 5, breakfasted at 8. About 11 passed a settlers shanty and at 2 stopped to lunch at settlement, bought some excellent bread and some cucumbers from a very witty little girl. "Indian azalia a la june hid in the desert." Settlements now became pretty numerous though I cannot say the log huts looked at all promising. About 7 came in sight of Fort Gratiot Light House. Entered the River St. Clair soon after 8. "Good bye Lake Huron." Passed Gratiot and crossed to our own shores again, landing at Port Sarnia at 9; our formidable appearance occasioned our being challenged and nearly fired into by the Militia, however in time we convinced them we were not Yankees and were allowed to land. Got a supply of apples.

Sketch of Fort Gratiot Lighthouse. The lighthouse, located at Port Huron, is still keeping watch over ships plying the St. Clair River. *Courtesy artist Steve McLean.*

3 September

Stay here all day. A famous breakfast, fresh eggs and c+c. Sarnia is a very pretty place. A small village perhaps 50 houses facing the stream and their cottages straggle a long way along the banks with pretty little gardens round them. The beautiful river winding magestically between rather higher banks then before and

Fort Gratiot, Michigan (1839). Only ruins remain in a small park, a remembrance of this once important, strategically positioned fort. *Courtesy Michigan State Archives and the Library of Congress.*

graceful vessels skimming along. I am quite delighted with the place. Just opposite is Fort Gratiot,[48] a whitewashed square of buildings surrounded by slight stone work exactly like Fort Brady. A few hundred yards below is a pretty large village, a railway runs from it to the head of the Grand River rapids (Michigan). Numbers of steamers ply up and down. The American village is called Port Huron and a small stream called the Black river runs into the River St. Clair. On our own side opposite the lighthouse at Point Edward there is an excellent fishery. In Sarnia there is a church but no clergyman, 3 or four excellent stores, an ice house and two taverns, and all sorts of vegetables grow in great abundance. After luncheoning at a Militia Officers station I

48 Fort Gratiot, or Fort St. Joseph as it was orginally called, was established by the French as early as 1686 when it played an important role in maintaining a strong French presence in the region. The fort was reinforced during the War of 1812 under the direction of Capt. Gratiot, an engineering officer, and his name was given to the fort. Troops were stationed there throughout the 1820s and 1830s, although it appears that the fort played no role in the events of 1837-38. For more on the history of this fort see, "History of Fort Gratiot," *Michigan Historical Collections*. Vol. 18, 1892.

looked into an Indian Council being held. Not above 20 present chiefly engrossed with the subject of the division of some sale money. I afterwards called on the Miss Jones, daughters of the Indian Agent, half French, funny girls; and then strolled along the main looking into a number of the settlements. Our party bagged a few partidges, some bitterns and a black squirrel. One or two gentleman dined with us and we had a very jovial evening, song and punch till 2 a.m.

4 September

Reduced one of our canoes, started at 2 down the river, there is some satisfaction here in really seeing that our side has much the advantage [over] our go-ahead neighbours which I am sorry to say is seldom the case. There are very excellent houses and fields, grain and pasture the whole way for many miles. About 8 miles down is Palmer, the Yankee county town, and nearby we stopped at Sutherlands Landing, the gentleman whom it is called after and owns it met us on the wharf and insisted on our coming to his house which we were by no means loath to close with. He is a regular character—quite a pickwick[49] and he gave us an excellent lunch which we did much justice to. It was also gratifying to perceive that our distinction of his ham and c+c and rapid draining of his cellar and brandy cask seemed to give him the greatest satisfaction ___ ___ evening arrived at 9 at the Baldoon farm[50] not at all sorry to get into a house.

---

49 Pickwick is likely a reference to Mr. Pickwick in Dicken's *Pickwick Papers* and used in the sense of being jovial, plump, etc.
50 In 1803, Lord Selkirk was granted 1,200 acres, part of a plan to settle Gaelic-speaking Highlanders in Southern Upper Canada. The settlement of Baldoon consisted of 950 acres of largely low-lying wetland, strategically placed near the passage between lakes Huron and St. Clair. The settlement had a short and troubled history, plagued by outbreaks of malaria, heavy rains and mismanagement. Lord Selkirk's connection to the settlement ended in 1818 when the Executive Council decided the project had failed and that the region should be opened to settlement. For a detailed discussion of Selkirk's Baldoon Settlement see, Fred Coyne Hamil, "Lord Selkirk in Upper Canada," *Ontario History*. Vol. XXXVII. 1945. 35-48; and Fred Coyne Hamil and Terry Jones, "The Story of Baldoon" *Ontario History*. Vol. LVII. No. 1. March 1965. 1-12.

5 September

The Baldoon farm was with a great tract of land the property of Lord Selkirk[51] and he established here a sheepwalk on a very huge scale. In the war however he had to drive as many as he could inland. ___ ___ was of course destroyed.[52] After this it was farmed and cultivated with great success when by the extraordinary rise of their lakes and their rivers it was flooded, withal even ___ ___ that was fine hard pasture land which is now as agueish looking a marsh as can be imagined. There are great quantities of game here. Our party bagged upwards of 100 duck and lost about an equal number. You have to wade away often 3 or 4 feet deep through the bull rushes for a day or two as you can depend on glorious sport. This as try wills, but I pity the poor wretch endeavored to live here. Buchanan shot a deer and saw several others and pigeon, duck, wood cock, bitterns and squirrels are very plentiful. We are most comfortable occupying the upper rooms of the large farm house originally built by Lord Selkirk.[53] Mr. Keating[54] came down to us and a Mr. Feythorne, an oxfordshire gentleman who has settled on Lake St. Clair. Rainy night.

6 September

Went 7 miles up the river with Col. Jarvis to Walpole Island

51 Thomas Douglas, 5th Earl of Selkirk, was born at Kirkcudbright in southwestern Scotland. Lord Selkirk was an avid supporter of Highland emigration at a time when most landlords, industrialists and the government were opposed. He established a relatively successful settlement in Prince Edward Island in 1803, undertook the Baldoon Settlement on the shores of Lake St. Clair, Upper Canada, and is best known for his ambitious settlement at Red River, Manitoba (1812). For a complete examination of the life of Lord Selkirk see, John Morgan Gray, *Lord Selkirk of Red River*. (Toronto: MacMillan, 1964).
52 During the War of 1812, Baldoon was plundered by American troops and its sheep driven to Detroit. The sheep were returned after the fall of Detroit; however, 118 of the flock were missing. Hamil and Jones, "Story of Baldoon," 11.
53 Lord Selkirk supervised the construction of the mansion house at Baldoon during his stay there in June of 1804. Ibid, 2-3.
54 This is in all likeliehood Mr. F. W. Keating, an Indian agent, who in 1843 expropriated £200 from funds of the Chenail Ecarte and Lake St. Clair Indian bands.

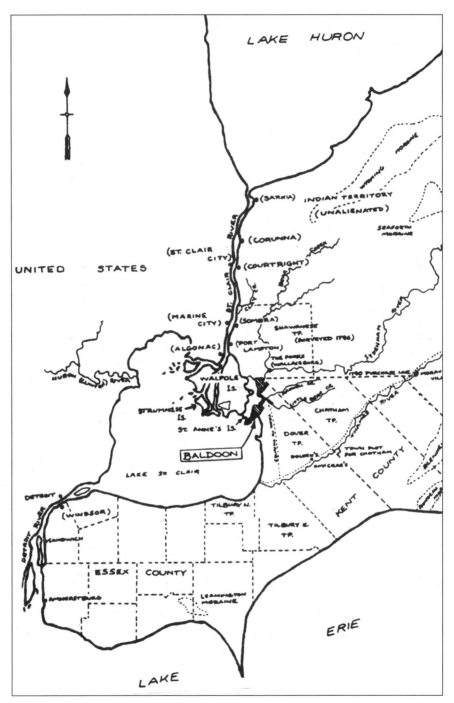

Map of the Baldoon Settlement. In 1804, fifteen families from Scotland settled near the St. Clair River in a community sponsored by Lord Selkirk. This ill-fated settlement ended in 1818, when the few remaining settlers moved to higher ground. Based on a map by Lloyd Clark, "The Baldoon Settlement Land Grants," Unpublished, 1970.

Grand Indian Council.[55] Many complaints of Yankee settlers. The general ___ of the river had occasioned much damage to the unfortunate settlers on the banks. Walpole Island is in some parts very pretty, even parklike. Oak trees growing ___ ___. Back at 4. A pleasant dinner consisting of soup, venison, wild duck, partridge, snipe and woodcock and a brandy water ___.

7 September

Beautiful morning. Up before 6. Down the river. Most dismal. Marshy on either side but thousands of ducks. Entered Lake St. Clair, and ___ 7 miles west of the mouth of the Thames (N.Tilbury). Ten moving along St. Clair and passed Hog and Peach Island, then at 7 passed Detroit on our right, Windsor on our left, and encamped at Sandwich at 8. A jovial evening with the 86th.

8 September

Crossed to Detroit in the forenoon. Very much pleased with the general appearance of the place. Lunched with the 85th and started

55 The native settlement on Walpole Island was begun at the end of the American War in 1783. The island was populated primarily by Chippewa of the Chenail Ecarte and Bear Creek bands, as well as Pottawatamies from Michigan State. A report of 1845 states that in 1842, presents were distributed to 1,140 Natives on the island. The same report notes that the Native settlement was having considerable problems with "...the profligate whites settled on the frontier, who, by various frauds and in moments of intoxication, obtained leases and took possession of the most fertile and valuable part of the island." John Richardson, *Tecumseh and Richardson: The Story of a Trip to Walpole Island and Port Sarnia*. (Toronto: Ontario Book Company, 1924) 105-107.

56 The settlement of Amherstburg was established as early as 1784, when the Huron and Ottawa bands who claimed the region, gave a tract of land at the mouth of the Detroit River to a group of British Officers whom they had fought alongside during the American War (1776-1783). It was recognized as being of strategic importance and over the years three separate forts were constructed in the region. The original fort was named Fort Amherstburg, but after reconstruction in 1839 the fort was renamed Fort Malden. For more on the early history of Amherstburg and Fort Malden see, C. C. James, *Early History of the Town of Amherstburg*. (Amherstburg: Echo Printing Co., 1902); and, Ernest J. Lajeunesse (ed.), *The Windsor Border Region*. (Toronto: University of Toronto Press, 1960) cxxi-cxxix.

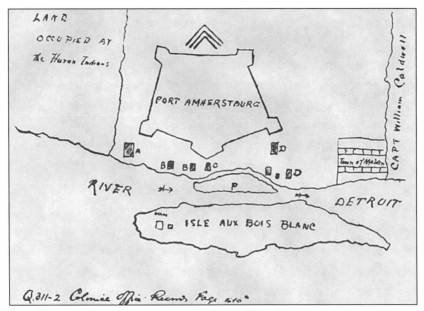

Sketch map of Fort Amherstburg showing the 1828 plan for the fort. From C. C. James, *Early History of the Town of Amherstburg*. (Amherstburg: Echo Printing Co. Ltd., 1902,) 14.

down the Detroit River at 2. Arrived at Amherstburg[56] at 4 and very hospitably ___ by H.M. 34th in the evening.[57]

9 September

Breakfast with 34th—left. Arrived at 3 in afternoon and down 18 miles to ___. Very well cleared country and beautiful orchards and large fields of Indian corn; all the family ___.

10 September

Off at 6 and down 15 miles to breakfast passing Point Pelee and

57 The 34th regiment had been stationed in Amherstburg during the summer of 1838 when filibustering along the border was threatening the peace of the region. R. M. Fuller, "The British Army: 34th Regiment of Foot on the Detroit River Frontier," *Western Ontario Historical Notes*. Vol.XIII, No.3. Sept. 1955. 18-19.
58 Lieutenant Agnew is referring to the rebel attack upon Point Pelee where about 400 Americans crossed the ice from Sandusky and took possession of Pelee Island. On March 2nd 1838, Colonel Maitland, with a detachment of royal artillery and companies of the 32nd and 83rd regiments stationed at Amherstburg, some volunteers and six natives, engaged the rebel force and drove them back across the river. The British force won the day but suffered considerable losses; the 32nd alone had two sergeants and twenty-eight rank and file wounded, and one corporal and three privates died of their wounds. Of the rebel force, one of their leaders and ten others were killed, at least thirty were wounded and reportedly many were drowned as they fled across the ice. T.R. *Invasions of Upper Canada from the United States: Battle of Point Au Pele*, (1841).

in sight of the island famous in 38 for the encounter with rebels[58] and found Mrs Wegle's a most excellent clean farm house rather than Inn. Fine country. Toward noon poorer sandy soil. Crossed the 5 mile wood and bagged 8 partridges. Beautiful woodland with loads of black squirrel. Brought up at ___ a ___ ___, a log house but very smug.

11 September

Off at 1/4 past 8. Great fun pigeon shooting.[59] Bagged five hare. Stopped 15 miles on to breakfast at ___ (rather an indifferent house). Excellent road. Then leaving the lake crossed the 10 mile wood, beautiful timber and then turning to the right entered a much more thriving country well cleared, excellent road. Bagged 7 brace more pigeon and stopped at Arain's Inn. A very nice clean comfortable house. Oxford township 39 miles.

12 September

Off at 6—Down 11 miles to breakfast to a very seedy rustic house kept by an Argyllshire gentleman, of course a Campbell. Fell in with a bevy of quail but only destroyed one. Some very deep gullies. About 2 came on Col. Talbots[60] property and could plainly observe a gradual improvement in the road when you get very near his place the woods are really beautiful fir, birch ___ to the very root—a beautiful valley extends north of his place and the

59 This was a time when the passenger pigeon still blackened the skies. In his diary, the author notes that on one occasion during the trip one member of their party killed 14 pigeons with one shot. Diary of Andrew Agnew, 1835-46. Edinburgh. Scottish Record Office. GD 154/780.

60 Colonel Thomas Talbot (1771-1853), the founder of the Talbot Settlement in Upper Canada and a member of the Legislative Council of Upper Canada. After military service in Canada and in Europe during the Napoleonic Wars, Talbot returned to Upper Canada and founded a settlement on a grant of 5,000 acres along Lake Erie. The settlement progressed slowly, until Talbot recognized the need for roads linking his townships with other settlements. Once road construction was implemented, settlement of the region developed rapidly. Here, he governed "...his settlers in almost patriarchal state, for nearly fifty years." W. Stewart Wallace (ed.), *The MacMillan Dictionary of Canadian Biography*. 3rd Edition. (London: MacMillan, 1963) 734. Also see, Gerald M. Craig, *Upper Canada: The Formative Years, 1784-1841*. (Toronto: McClelland and Stewart Limited, 1968), 142-144.

Detroit River, circa 1837. As early as the 1830s, the Detroit River was bustling with traffic. *The White Pigeon Republican* for May 15, 1839 lists thirty-three steamboats active on Lake Erie alone, and traffic between Detroit and Chicago increased with each passing year. *Courtesy Michigan State Archives.*

road exceeding the other sidewinds through beautiful parklike scenery. We stopped 3 miles further in at Water's Inn where we got an excellent dinner.

13 September

When we got up this morning the ground was perfectly white with hoar frost—a hint to the leaves of their approaching end. It was very fine though raining. A beautiful drive on excellent road 10 miles to St. Thomas—a dear little place stands very high and commands a very extensive view.[61] Breakfasted at the St. Thomas

61 The settlement of St. Thomas was founded in 1810 by Captain Daniel Rapelje from New York State. He built a grist mill and laid out his farm in lots, which he sold to settlers. In 1824 Dr. Charles Duncombe and Dr. John Rolph opened Upper Canada's first medical school here, which they called the Talbot Dispensatory. Duncombe was an ardent support of William Lyon Mackenzie's reform party and was forced to flee to the United States in 1837. David E. Scott, *Ontario Place Names.* (Vancouver: Whitecap Books, 1993) 193.

62 An early visitor to St. Thomas remarked that "...it was fortunate that St. Thomas had such a long main street so that it could accommodate all of its taverns." Wayne Paddon, *Steam and Petticoats.* (London: Murray Kelly Ltd., 1977) 162.

Hotel[62] and then drove on. Soon the beautiful hardwood is changed to tall, dull dreary looking pines and the soil becomes very sandy. Shot some pigeons; and were capably put up at a Mr. Bondsales.

14 September

Beautiful morning. Off at 6 and down to breakfast to London's hotel. Shot 2 brace of pigeons and a dozen partridge. Got an excellent breakfast and then walked over the old gentleman's orchard and grounds. Drove into Brantford at 9 p.m.

Sunday 15 September

To Hamilton through Ancaster. Beautiful situation.

16 September

Walked over Sir A. ___ "Chesters" ___ and ___ by train to Toronto at 7. Home again after a most jovial cruise of 8 weeks.

Andrew Agnew, Lieut. 93rd Highlanders

Epilogue

Having ended his eight week journey through Upper Canada and portions of Michigan, Lieutenant Andrew Agnew returned to garrison duty, refreshed from the adventure and in good health. Fort York was comfortable and, with winter fast approaching, preparations were being made for a quiet season. He believed that "a pleasanter quarter there certainly is not in America..."[1] and had already begun to hail the approach of Christmas with "libations of mulled port."[2] The border was peaceful, with little threat of raids the likes of which occurred during the previous year. However, despite the comfortable situation in which Lieutenant Agnew found himself, he was becoming increasingly dissatisfied with life in the colonies.

Lieutenant Agnew's correspondence provides evidence of his growing restlessness. In March of 1840, he wrote his father, from whom he regularly sought advice, and related that "...there is a good deal to see for two or three years..[but]... I have already run nearly out..."[3] With the trip through Upper Canada now at a close, Lieutenant Agnew now felt that he had experienced all that Upper Canada had to offer. He then began to turn his thoughts to transferring to another regiment, one preferably stationed in the Mediterranean or headed there, as he had yet to see that part of the world. India was also of interest. The 16th Lancers, he wrote, would be a perfect fit as:

> "I should have a free passage of course and see much of India, perhaps a little service which now a days is a great object indeed, the regiment went abroad in 1822 so that they would return to England at the latest about 1844;

Soldiers were frequently visible on the streets of garrison towns. This c. 1840 painting by John Gillespie depicts members of the 93rd Sutherlanders on King Street, Toronto, near the St. Lawrence Market. *Photograph courtesy Royal Ontario Museum,* ©ROM.

> when I should of course be brought back again gratis after having seen an immensity of the world..."[4]

Military service, at least in the eyes of Lieutenant Agnew, offered prospects of seeing the world.

There was, however, another reason Lieutenant Agnew began turning his mind to transferring to another regiment. Lieutenant Agnew found life in the colonies lacking, "...there is no recommendation in the way of society, polishing to the mind or manners..."[5] More significantly, he appears to have developed a certain uneasiness with the regiment, which he found lacked 'gentlemen.' Lieutenant Agnew got along 'tolerably well' with Colonel Sparks, the commander of the regiment, but also found him lacking in civility. Colonel Sparks was not, Agnew wrote his father in strictest confidence, 'born a gentleman.'[6] In short, Lieutenant Agnew found the regiment to lack the necessary society which he needed, something he believed he would find in a number of other regiments.

In April of 1841, Lieutenant Agnew's wishes came true. He was promoted to Captain and granted leave to return to Britain.

Fort York, established as a military post by Lieutenant-Governor John Graves Simcoe in 1793, was destroyed following an American attack (April 1813) during the War of 1812. Reconstruction begun in the summer of 1813 continued into 1816 and ultimately the garrison became home to the British regulars serving in Upper Canada, including members of Highland Regiments such as the one depicted in this illustration. *Courtesy National Archives of Canada.*

Before doing so, he embarked on a lengthy trip through the United States, stopping at New York, Philadelphia, Washington (where he saw the original Declaration of Independence), Baltimore and Boston. On May 16th he left Boston 'for the old country' stopping for a few weeks in Halifax and in St. John's New Brunswick before heading overseas.[7]

On the 8th of July, 1842, Captain Andrew Agnew received an exchange into the 4th Light Dragoons. On July 12 he briefly joined the regiment at Brighton, before 'selling out' of the army and returning home to Lochnaw. After a short stay, he again left home, this time to 'see the world.' His fourteen month journey abroad took him to Belgium, Germany, Switzerland and Italy; then on to Greece and Turkey before returning home. In 1845, at

Portrait of Sir Andrew Agnew in the early
1880s. *Courtesy Sir Crispin Agnew.*

the age of twenty seven, he married Lady Louisa Noel, daughter
of Charles, 1st Earl of Gainsborough. In 1849, he succeeded his
father, the well-known 'advocate and champion of the Sabbath'
as 8th Baronet of Lochnaw.[8]

The regiment which Captain Agnew had left behind in Upper
Canada experienced nothing comparable to his extensive travels.
They remained in Upper Canada until 1848, conducting garrison
duties and from time to time assisting the civil authorities in
some capacity. Upon returning home to Britain, the regiment was
first stationed at Stirling, many no doubt happy to be back in
Scotland after a decade of service overseas. In 1854, the regiment
would once again leave Britain, this time for service in Malta,
Gallipoli and the Crimea, where they would earn great honours

in the Battle of Balaclava.[9] The regiment attracted further honours in India for its part in the siege of Lucknow. In 1881, the 93rd and 91st Argyllshire regiments were amalgamated, forming the Princess Louise's Argyll and Sutherland Highlanders.

Notes

INTRODUCTION

1 Gourlay's idea was to produce a book on Upper Canada which would provide prospective emigrants with the necessary information on where and how to settle. The work was to be patterned on Sir John Sinclair's *Statistical Account of Scotland*, and like Sinclair, Gourlay proposed sending questionnaires throughout Upper Canada in order to gather the information he needed. See Lois Darroch Milani, *Robert Gourlay, Gadfly*. (Guelph: Ampersand Press, 1971) 75.

2 Robert E. Saunders has noted the difficulty of defining exactly what constituted the Family Compact, stating that it is impossible to go much further than to say "...they were the men who held government positions...those persons whom the reformers and their friends opposed." From "The Family Compact Defined," in *The Family Compact: Aristocracy or Oligarchy*. David W. L. Earl, (ed.) (Toronto: C. Clark Publishing Co. 1967) 16.

3 T. H. Raddall, *Path of Destiny*. (Toronto: Doubleday 1957) 372-374. For a complete study of Robert Gourlay and the events leading up to his banishment see, Milani, *Robert Gourlay, Gadfly*. 74-215.

4 The *Colonial Advocate* first appeared in May, 1824. Mackenzie printed 800 copies and mailed them at his expense to prospective subscribers in Upper Canada, Great Britain and the United States. Initially, the paper provided readers with an assortment of information on agriculture, trade and manufacturing, letters, news and advertisements. However, over time it became more political and focused more upon challenging those in power. See David Flint, *William Lyon Mackenzie: Rebel Against Authority*. (Toronto: Oxford University Press 1971) 21- 27.

5 Louis Joseph Papineau (1786-1872) was a prominent political figure in Lower Canada before leading the French-Canadian reformers or *Patriotes*. He was a forceful voice in the reform movement in Lower Canada but took no active part in the actual rebellion, choosing to flee to the United States where he remained until 1839. He would later move to Paris, France, where he lived until 1844, at which time he returned to Lower Canada and re-entered politics. W. Stewart Wallace (ed.), *The MacMillan Dictionary of Canadian Biography*. Third Edition. (London: MacMillan, 1963) 576.

6 Mackenzie claimed to have 4,000 to 5,000 volunteers ready to fight, yet when he began his march on Toronto, his force consisted of several hundred men. Most of these were settlers from north of Toronto who were unprepared for actual battle. Flint, *William Lyon Mackenzie, Rebel Against Authority*. 136-137.

7 Raddall, *Path of Destiny*. 383.

8 J. MacKay Hitsman, *Safeguarding Canada*. (Toronto: University of Toronto Press, 1968) 132.

9 For more on the proclamation of neutrality and the position of the United States on this and related issues see Albert B. Corey, *The Crisis of 1830-1842 in Canadian American Relations*. (New York: Russell and Russell, 1970) 50-57.

10 Raddall states that estimates ran as high as 200,000 members in both the United States and Upper and Lower Canada. *Path of Destiny*, 397-399.

11 In the two decades following the establishment of the regiment in 1799, Sutherland and its surrounding counties supplied the majority of new recruits. During this period, 220 out of 688 recruits originated in Sutherland. Caithness (24), Ross (47), Inverness (50) and Fife (98) also figured prominently. Henderson points out that Sutherland men provided the nucleus of NCO's and Sergeants and therefore had an important role to play within the regiment. *Highland Soldier*. (Edinburgh: John Donald Publishers, 1989) 54.

12 Roderick Hamilton Burgoyne, *Historical Records of the 93rd Sutherland Highlanders*. (London: R. Bentley, 1883) 3.

13 Henderson cites the fact that during the period 1799 to 1819, not a single individual of the Light Company received punishment. *Highland Soldier*, 60.

14 Henderson sees this as being a combination of a variety of factors, including: more widespread recruiting, the discharge of all the original recruits, a less personal relationship between the land and service. *Highland Soldier*, 60-61. Hew Strachan has suggested that from the 1830s, Scots were increasingly reluctant to join the army and that many shied away from joining a Highland Regiment on account of their not wanting to wear the kilt, or at least pay for the added expense it took to purchase and maintain such an outfit. *The Reform of the British Army, 1830- 1854*. (Manchester, Manchester University Press, 1984) 51.

15 Captain Charles Gordon, "Record of the Services of the 93rd (or Sutherland) Highland Regt. of Foot." (Guelph, University of Guelph Archives) MSS. XSIMSA103.

16 Burgoyne states that the *Pique* encountered "...one of the most boisterous passages across the Atlantic that any individual on board had ever experienced." The result was that the ship did not make Halifax harbour until the

6th of March. Burgoyne, *Historical Records of the 93rd Sutherland Highlanders,* 73.

17 Hew Strachan, *The Reform of the British Army.* (Manchester: Manchester University Press, 1984) 58-60.

18 What made matters worse was that in the colonies regimental canteens were operated by private contractors who would extend credit to soldiers they were only too willing to exploit. Peter Burroughs, "Crime and Punishment in the British Army, 1815-1870," *English Historical Review.* Vol.C. No.396. (London: Longman Group Ltd. July, 1986) 555.

19 As one writer noted in 1835, " If drunkenness alone was the result of drinking I should not, perhaps, say what I do; but to gratify that passion the soldiers sell their necessaries, and when in a state of intoxication become insubordinate, and are as ready to knock down officers as serjeants; in fine, it leads to a variety of crimes, and, unfortunately, to a repetition of them." As quoted in Burroughs, "Crime and Punishment in the British Army, 1815-1870," 556.

20 See, J. R. Dinwiddy, "The Early Nineteenth-Century Campaign against flogging in the Army," *English Historical Review.* Vol. XCVII. (London: Longman Group Ltd., 1982) 308-331; and Peter Burroughs, "Crime and Punishment in the British Army, 1815-1870," 545-571.

21 This included better provisions for married soldiers, improved barracks, reading libraries and savings banks, among other measures. Ibid, 57-75.

22 National Archives of Canada, Ottawa. War Office Records. Letter dated Toronto, 11th Nov. 1839. 'C' Series. 1007. 20-23.

23 In a letter of 30th November, 1841 (Montreal) Colonel Sparks was applying for fuel and light for the regiments library. National Archives of Canada, Ottawa. War Office Records. 'C' Series. 1007. 63. The foundation of regimental libraries was at first unpopular, many commanders fearing that "Too good an education would make all soldiers potential officers and they would therefore be discontented with their lot as privates." Strachan, *The Reform of the British Army,* 89.

24 "Letter to Lieut. Colonel Eden," dated Citadel Barracks, Quebec. 24th January, 1833. National Archives of Canada, Ottawa. War Office Records. RG8 C2775 "C" Series. Vol. 171.

25 Ibid. Also see, Peter Burroughs, "Tackling Army Desertion in British North America," *Canadian Historical Review.* Vol. LXI. 1980, 35.

26 Mary Beacock Fryer, *Battlefields of Canada.* (Toronto: Dundurn Press, 1986) 191.

27 Nils von Schoultz is an interesting character. He claimed to be an exile from

Poland, where he had served as an officer in the Polish army and worked as a chemist. He gained American sympathies for his cause by comparing the Canadians to the Polish peasants who suffered under Russian domination. In reality, he was a Finnish-born Swedish national who had briefly held a commission in the Polish army. Unable to support his wife and daughter, he left for England, and then embarked for New York where he passed himself off as an experienced chemist. At the time of the raid on Prescott, he was engaged to be married to a woman in Syracuse, New York. Mary Beacock Fryer, *Battlefields of Canada*. (Toronto: Dundurn Press, 1986) 193-194.

28 Lieutenant Andrew Agnew, "Letter dated Toronto, Upper Canada. December 8th, 1838. Edinburgh. Scottish Record Office. GD.154/745/6 (1-2).

29 Ibid.

30 Subsequent reports listed 56 Patriot casualties and 16 wounded. George F. G. Stanley, "The Battle of the Windmill." *Historic Kingston*. No.3. November 1954. 47.

31 Lieutenant Andrew Agnew, Letter dated Toronto, December 8th. 1838. Edinburgh. Scottish Record Office. G.D. 154/745/6 (1-2)

32 Elinor Kyte Senior, *British Regulars in Montreal*. (Montreal, McGill-Queens University Press 1981) 70.

33 Letter dated Montreal, 4th October 1845. Ottawa, National Archives of Canada. War Office Records. RG8 C2872 Vol.316. 392-394.

34 "General Orders," dated Headquarters, Montreal, 14th October, 1845. Ottawa, National Archives of Canada. War Office Records. RG8 C3508 1448.

35 John Philp, "The Economic and Social Effects of the British Garrisons on the Development of Western Upper Canada," *Ontario History*. Vol.XLI. No.I. 1949. 48.

36 Letter dated Toronto, Upper Canada. 8th December 1838. Edinburgh. Scottish Record Office. GD. 154/745/16 (1-2).

37 The fact that Lieutenant Agnew was an officer and a member of Scotland's landed class also meant that he was used to a different lifestyle than many, and therefore could complain of such things as the "bad brandy" available in the colonies. "Letter dated Brighton, Upper Canada. 8th July, 1839. Edinburgh. Scottish Record Office. GD 134/745/10

38 Peter S. Schmalz, *The Ojibwa of Southern Ontario*. (Toronto: University of Toronto Press, 1991) 131-132.

39 "Letter dated Brighton, Upper Canada. 8th July, 1839. Edinburgh. Scottish Record Office. GD 134/745/10.

40 Ibid.

EPILOGUE

1 Letter of Andrew Agnew dated Toronto, Upper Canada. 8 November 1839. Edinburgh, Scottish Record Office. GD 154/745/12.

2 Ibid.

3 Letter of Andrew Agnew dated Toronto, Upper Canada, March 9, 1840. Edinburgh, Scottish Record Office. GD154/745/14 (1-2).

4 Ibid.

5 Ibid.

6 Letter of Andrew Agnew dated Toronto, Upper Canada. November 8th, 1839. Edinburgh, Scottish Record Office. GD 154/745/12.

7 "Diary of Andrew Agnew, 1835-1846," Edinburgh, Scottish Record Office. GD 154/780.

8 Thomas McCrie, *Memoirs of Sir Andrew Agnew of Lochnaw*. (London, 1850) 80.

9 R. H. Burgoyne, *Historical Records of the 93rd Sutherland Highlanders*. (London, R. Bentley 1883) 94-126.

Bibliography

Agnew, Andrew, "Journal of Tour From Toronto to Manitoulin Island, 1839," Edinburgh. Scottish Record Office. GD154/783.
—"Diary of Andrew Agnew, 1835–1846," Edinburgh. Scottish Record Office. GD   154/780.
—"Letter Dated 25th September, 1839," Edinburgh. Scottish Record Office. GD.   154/745/11 (14).

Bradford, Robert D., *Historic Forts Ontario*. Belleville: Mika Publishing Co., 1988.

Burden, Harold Nelson, *Manitoulin; or Five Years of Church Work Among Ojibwa Indians and Lumbermen*. London: Simpkin, Marshall, Hamilton, Kent: 1895.

Burgoyne, Roderick Hamilton, *Historical Records of the 93rd Sutherland Highlanders*. London: R. Bentley, 1883.

Burroughs, Peter, "Tackling Army Desertion in British North America," *Canadian Historical Review*. Vol. LXI No. 1. March, 1980.

Burroughs, Peter, "Crime and Punishment in the British Army, 1815–1870," *English Historical Review*. Vol. C. No. 396. July, 1985.

Chute, Janet E., *The Legacy of Singwaukonse: A Century of Native Leadership*. Toronto: University of Toronto Press, 1998.

Corey, Albert B. *The Crisis of 1830–1842 in Canadian-American Relations*. New York: Russell and Russell, 1970.

Craig, Gerald M. (ed.), *Early Travellers in the Canadas, 1791–1867*. Toronto: MacMillan, 1955.

Craig, Gerald M. (ed.), *Upper Canada: The Formative Years, 1784–1841*. Toronto. McClelland and Stewart Ltd: 1968.

Detroit Free Press, "History of Fort Gratiot," *Michigan Historical Collections*. Vol. 18. 1892.

Dinwiddy, J.R., "The Early Nineteenth-century Campaign Against Flogging in the Army," *English Historical Review*. Vol.XCVII. 1982.

Dunham, Aileen, *Political Unrest in Upper Canada, 1815–1836*. Toronto: McClelland and Stewart Ltd., 1963.

Flint, David, *William Lyon Mackenzie: Rebel Againsty Authority*. Toronto: Oxford University Press, 1971.

Fuller, R.M., "The British Army: 34th Regiment of Foot on the Detroit River Frontier," *Western Ontario Historical Notes*. Vol.XIII, No. 3. Sept. 1955.

Fryer, Mary Beacock, *Battlefields of Canada*. Toronto: Dundurn Press, 1986.

Gordon, Charles, "Record of the Services of the 93rd (or Sutherland) Highland Regt. Of Foot," *Scottish Collection*. University of Guelph. MSS. XS1MSA103.

Gourlay, Robert, "The Oligarchy Attacked," *The Family Compact: Aristocracy or Oligarchy?* David W.L. Earl (ed.), Toronto: C. Clark Publishing Company, 1967.

Hamil, Fred Coyne, "Lord Selkirk in Upper Canada," *Ontario History*. Vol. XXXVII. 1945.

Hamil, Fred Coyne and Terry Jones, "The Story of Baldoon," *Ontario History*. Vol. LVII. No. 1. March, 1965.

Harris, R. Cole (ed.), *Historical Atlas of Canada: From Beginning to 1800*. Toronto: University of Toronto Press, 1987.

Henderson, Diana, *Highland Soldier*. Edinburgh: John Donald Publishers, 1989.

Henry, Alexander, *Travels and Adventures in Canada and the Indian Territories*. James Bain (ed.), Rutland, Vermont: C.E. Tuttle Co., 1969.

Hitsman, J. Mackay, *Safeguarding Canada*. Toronto: University of Toronto Press, 1968.

James, C.C., *Early History of the Town of Amherstburg*. Amherstburg, Ont.: Echo Printing Company Limited, 1902.

Jameson, Anna, *Winter Studies and Summer Rambles in Canada*. Toronto: McClelland and Stewart, 1923.

Jury, Elsie McLeod, *The Establishments at Penetanguishene*. Bulletin No.12. London: University of Western Ontario, 1959.

Kilbourn, William, *The Firebrand*. Toronto: Clarke, Irwin and Company Ltd., 1956.

Lajeunesse, Ernest J. (ed.), *The Windsor Border Region*. Toronto: University of Toronto Press, 1960.

Landon, Fred, "British Regiments in London," *Western Ontario Historical Notes*. Vol.XIII, No. 3. Sept. 1955.

Lewis, Rendall M., "The Manitoulin Letters of the Rev. Charles Crosbie Brough," *Ontario History*. Vol. XLVIII. No. 2. 1956.

Lytwyn, Victor P., "Ojibwa and Ottawa Fisheries Around Manitoulin Island: Historical and Geographical Perspectives on Aboriginal and Treaty Fishing Rights," *Native Studies Review*. 6. No.1. (1990).

MacKenzie, A.E.D., *Baldoon*. Petrolia: Phelps Publishing Co., 1978.

Mackerlie, Peter H., *History of the Lands and Their Owners in Galloway*. Vol. 1. Edinburgh: W. Paterson, 1870.

M'Crie, Thomas, *Memoirs of the Life of Sir Andrew Agnew of Lochnaw*. Edinburgh: 1850.

Milani, Lois Darroch, *Robert Gourlay, Gadfly*. Guelph: Ampersand Press, 1971.

Morris, J.A., *Prescott, 1810–1967*. Prescott: The Prescott Journal, 1967.

Munro, William, *Manitoulin Echoes, From Bluff, Dale, Lake and Stream*. Gore Bay: The Recorder Press, 1900.

Murdoch, Su, "The Wish to Take a Sketch of It: George Hallen and Family," *East Georgian Bay Historical Journal*. Vol. II. 1982.

Pacey, Elizabeth, *Halifax Citadel*. Halifax: Parks Canada, 1985.

Paddon, Wayne, *Steam and Petticoats*. London: Murray Kelly Ltd., 1977.

Pearen, Shelley J., *Exploring Manitoulin*. Toronto: University of Toronto Press, 1992.

Perkins, Mary Ellen, *A Guide to Provincial Plaques in Ontario*. Toronto: Natural Heritage/Natural History Inc., 1989.

Philp, John, "The Economic and Social Effects of the British Garrisons on the Development of Western Upper Canada," *Ontario History*. Vol. XLI. No.1. Toronto: 1949.

Raddall, T.H., *The Path of Destiny*. Toronto: Doubleday, 1957.

Richardson, John, *Tecumseh and Richardson: The Story of a Trip to Walpole Island and Port Sarnia*. Toronto: Ontario Book Company, 1924.

Rowe, Mrs. S. "Anderson Record, From 1699–1896," *Ontario Historical Society, Papers and Records*. Vol. VI. Toronto: 1905.

Salutin, Rick, *1837*. Toronto: James Lorimer and Company, 1976.

Saunders, R.E., "The Family Compact Defined," *The Family Compact: Aristocracy or Oligarchy?* Ed. David W.L. Earl. Toronto: C. Clark Publishing Company, 1967.

Schmalz, Peter S., *The Ojibwa of Southern Ontario*. Toronto: University of Toronto Press, 1991.

Scott, David E. *Ontario Placenames*. Vancouver: Whitecap Books, 1993.

Senior, Elinor Kyte, *British Regulars in Montreal*. Montreal: McGill-Queens University Press, 1981.

Skelley, Alan Ramsay, *The Victorian Army at Home*. London: Croom Helm, 1977.

_____, "Sketches of Long Ago," *Michigan Historical Collections*. V.14. 1895.

Smith, Donald, *Sacred Feathers*. Toronto: University of Toronto Press, 1987.

Spiers, Edward M., *The Army and Society 1815–1914*. London: Longman, 1980.

Stanley, George F.G., "The Battle of the Windmill," *Historic Kingston*. No. 3. Nov. 1954.

Strachan, Hew, *The Reform of the British Army, 1830–1854*. Manchester: Manchester University Press, 1984.

Talbot, Edward Allan, "Gourlay and Upper Canadian Society," *The Family Compact: Aristocracy or Oligarchy?* Ed. David W.L. Earl. Toronto: C. Clark Publishing Company, 1967.

T.R. , *Invasions of Upper Canada From the United States: Battle of Point Au Pele, 1841.*

Wallace, W. Stewart (ed.), *The MacMillan Dictionary of Canadian Biography*. Third Edition. London: MacMillan, 1963.

War Office, "General Orders," dated Headquarters, Montreal, 14th October, 1845. RG8 C3508 1448.

War Office, "Letter to Lieut. Colonel Eden," Dated Citadel Barracks, Quebec. 24th January, 1833. RG8 C2775. "C" Series. Vol. 171.

Waterston, Elizabeth, *The Travellers-Canada to 1900*. Guelph: University of Guelph, 1989.

Wells, Kenneth McNeill, *Cruising the Georgian Bay*. Toronto: Kingswood House, 1958.

Wood, Stephen, *The Scottish Soldier*. Manchester: National Museums of Scotland, 1987.

Suggested Reading

There are a wide variety of related works which might prove of interest. Numerous travellers published accounts of their travels through Upper Canada during the 1830s and 1840s. Most relevant to the present work is Anna Jameson's, *Winter Studies and Summer Rambles in Canada*. 3 Vol. London: 1839. Other works which provide excellent descriptions of Upper Canada in the 1820s and 1830s include Adam Fergusson's, *Practical Notes Made During a Tour in Canada, and a Portion of the United States, in 1831*. Edinburgh: 1833; "A Backwoodsman" (William Dunlop) in *Statistical Sketches of Upper Canada*. London:1832; and John Galt's *Autobiography*. 2 Vol. London: 1833. Galt, the famous Scottish novelist and head of the Canada Company, did not publish his Canadian travels, but included much of them in his *Autobiography*, including his visit to Penetanguishene, Georgian Bay and the Lake Huron shore. An earlier, but relevant and highly entertaining work is Alexander Henry's, *Travels and Adventures in Canada and the Indian Territories*. James Bain (ed.) Toronto: 1901.

There are a wide range of works on the British Military both at home and abroad which might be consulted. One of the better studies of the Highland Regiments remains Diana Henderson's, *Highland Soldier*. Edinburgh: 1989. Stephen Wood, *The Scottish Soldier*. Manchester: 1987, is also an excellent work; in particular see chapter five, "The Wellington Years." The most detailed study of the 93rd remains R.H. Burgoyne's, *Historical Records of the 93rd Sutherland Highlanders*. London: 1883. While dated and written in the style of a nineteenth century regimental history, it is very detailed and provides an excellent framework for further studies of the regiment. For works examining army life and the changing nature of the British military in the early nineteenth century see: Hew Strachan, *The Reform of the British Army: 1830-54*. Manchester: 1984; Richard L. Blanco, "Reform and Wellington's Post-Waterloo Army, 1815-1854," *Military Affairs*. Vol. XXIX, 1965; Peter Burroughs, "Crime and Punishment in the British Army, 1815–1870," *English Historical Review*. Vol. C. No.396. July 1985; J.R. Dinwiddy, "The Early Nineteenth-Century Campaign Against Flogging in the Army," *English Historical Review*. Vol. XCVII. 1982; and Edward M. Spiers, *The Army and Society, 1815–1914*. New York: 1980.

For works focusing upon the British Army in British North America see: Elinor Kyte Senior, *British Regulars in Montreal*. Montreal: 1981; Elizabeth Pacey,

Halifax Citadel. Halifax: 1985; J. Mackay Hitsman, *Safeguarding Canada, 1763–1871*. Toronto: 1968; Peter Burroughs, "Tackling Army Desertion in British North America," *Canadian Historical Review*. Vol. LXI.1980; Fred Landon, "British Regiments in London," *Western Ontario Historical Notes*. Vol. XVIII, No. 3. September 1955; and John Philp, "The Economic and Social Effects of the British Garrisons on the Development of Western Upper Canada," *Ontario History*. Vol. XLI. No. I. Toronto: 1949. For an excellent guide to sources on the British soldier in Canada see: Timothy Dube, "Tommy Atkins, We Never Knew Ye: Documenting the British Soldier in Canada, 1759–1871," *Canadian Military History*. Vol. 4. No. I. Spring 1995.

Index

About the Editor

Scott A. McLean has a PhD in Scottish History and is presently living in Owen Sound, Ontario. Scott has been teaching in the Scottish Studies Department of the University of Guelph and, recently, has taught at Queen's International Study Centre at Herstmonceux Castle, East Sussex, England. He served as General Editor of the journal *Scottish Tradition* (1991–1998) and acted as Coordinator of the Office of Scottish Studies at the University of Guelph. He has published a variety of articles on Medieval and Modern Scotland and is presently researching works on the Scottish periodical press and Scottish emigration to Upper Canada.